Paul Forrester

GOURMET IRELAND
TWO

GOURMET IRELAND
TWO

Paul and Jeanne Rankin

BBC BOOKS

NOTE FOR VEGETARIANS
Recipes suitable for vegetarians are marked with a (V) symbol. Please note
that these may include cheese and other dairy products.

This book is published to accompany the second
Gourmet Ireland television series,
produced by Brian Waddell Productions
and first shown on BBC2 in 1995.
Executive Producer: Brian Waddell
Director: Stephen Stewart

Published by BBC Books,
an imprint of BBC Worldwide Publishing,
BBC Worldwide Limited,
Woodlands, 80 Wood Lane,
London W12 0TT

First published 1995
© Paul and Jeanne Rankin 1995

The moral rights of the authors have been asserted.

ISBN 0 563 37163 3

Designed by Mason Linklater
Drawings by Ivan Allen
Photographs by Graham Kirk
Styling by Helen Payne

Set in Berkeley Old Style
Printed and bound in Great Britain by BPC,
Paulton Books Limited, Paulton
Colour separations by Radstock Reproductions, Midsomer Norton
Jacket printed by Lawrence Allen Limited, Weston-super-Mare

Contents

ACKNOWLEDGEMENTS

We would like to thank our producer Brian Waddell and our director Stephen Stewart for their encouragement and direction during the making of the second *Gourmet Ireland* television series. All of the film crew were absolutely wonderful.

Our admiration for the artisans of this island and gratitude for all that they are doing in the name of food is hard to put into words. There are so many individuals doing such amazing things. All we can say is keep it up. Your work is noticed and appreciated.

We also want to mention the photographer Graham Kirk and his stylist Helen Payne. They have done a terrific job on both books and are a real pleasure to work with.

And, of course, once again we want to thank the staff members back at *Roscoff*, our restaurant in Belfast. We could never have done this without their hard work and support.

P & JR

INTRODUCTION

When we were travelling around Ireland for the first series of *Gourmet Ireland*, we discovered many exciting people who were growing and creating all sorts of delicious food products, both traditional and alternative. On our journey for the second series, we found that these artisans were growing in number and in knowledge. How could we not be inspired? There is a wealth of fresh produce, healthy crops, truly organic game, and bountiful fish and seafood in the country waiting to be enjoyed. Irish food will not stand still. Just as American cuisine has embraced exciting seasonings, and new cooking techniques and concepts in its resurgence, so Irish food is evolving all the time. We believe that in a few years' time it will be totally accepted, in the same way that British food prepared with British products has been.

For many of us, it's only when there is a special occasion to celebrate, or when we have some friends to entertain, that we really make time to put together an appealing three-course meal. We've created these menus for just those sorts of occasion. We also, however, chose them as showcases for the tremendous products that you can find in Ireland. As a result, some of them are a little one-sided, so you should feel absolutely free to mix and match. You can liven up a 'Lean Times' menu by including a hearty dish from 'Country Fare', or add some indulgence from 'Cupid's Cuisine' to a 'Family Get Together'. You can also, of course, try out individual dishes. Remember, though, that you should always be guided by what's in season and by what's in your cupboard.

This book reflects one of our own particular interests which is healthy eating. Today there is much more awareness of what foods actually do to and for us than there was in the past, and there is a much greater demand for nutritional information. People want light meals which are both good for them and easy to prepare. Vegetarianism is rapidly growing in popularity, while red meat eaters are turning more to white meat and other lean alternatives than before.

Healthy eating doesn't have to mean a strict regime, nor does it mean cutting out natural foods like cream and butter. It's all a question of balance. Natural products, treated respectfully, will always be better for you than processed foodstuffs. The cooking method - for example, deep-fat frying or steaming - can make or break the healthiness of a meal. Although there are a few decadent dishes in the following chapters - and everyone should feel free to indulge themselves without guilt sometimes - most of the ideas tend to go in a healthier direction. So if you find these dishes fresh, tasty and interesting, then you can be pretty sure that they are good for you too.

CHAPTER 1

CATCH OF THE DAY

IRELAND, SURROUNDED BY THE OCEAN AND WITH LOUGHS AND RIVERS TEEMING WITH FISH, IS ONE OF THE BEST PLACES ON EARTH TO ENJOY FISH AND SEAFOOD DISHES. BUT WHEREVER YOU LIVE FIND A TRUSTY FISHMONGER AND THEN TRY OUT SOME OF THESE RECIPES.

MENU 1

Smoked Eel Pâté with Fresh Herbs
......

Roast Fillet of Brill with Potato Scales
......

Warm Leek Vinaigrette
......

Chocolate Roulade with Raspberries
......

MENU 2

Risotto Molly Malone
......

Steamed Hake with Sliced Tomatoes and Tarragon
......

Roast Bananas with Waffles
......

SMOKED EEL PÂTÉ WITH FRESH HERBS

CONSIDERING HOW POPULAR EELS ARE ON THE CONTINENT AND THE MANY DELICIOUS WAYS THEY CAN BE COOKED, WE FIND IT AMAZING THAT MOST FOLK IN IRELAND SEEM TO BE SCARED TO DEATH OF THEM. PERHAPS IT'S THEIR SNAKE-LIKE APPEARANCE - HOW COULD SOMETHING THAT LOOKS LIKE THAT TASTE GOOD? WE THINK THEY'RE GREAT, AND THIS PÂTÉ WOULD MAKE A FINE RECIPE FOR CONVERTING ANY UNBELIEVERS. SERVE IT WITH TOAST, OR DELICIOUS IRISH WHEATEN BREAD (PAGE 89). IF YOU CAN'T FIND SMOKED EEL, THIS RECIPE WORKS BEAUTIFULLY WITH SMOKED MACKEREL.

SERVES 6-8

1.25 kg (2¹/₂ lb) whole smoked eel or 550 g (1¹/₄ lb) eel fillets
150 g (5 oz) unsalted butter, softened
1 tablespoon Dijon mustard
2 tablespoons chopped fresh parsley
2 tablespoons snipped fresh chives
2 tablespoons chopped fresh dill
1 tablespoon small capers, rinsed
6 tablespoons lemon juice
¹/₄ teaspoon cayenne pepper
1 hard-boiled egg yolk
salt and freshly ground black pepper
salad leaves to garnish (optional)

To skin the eel, simply break off the head, pulling backwards and downwards. Don't separate the head from the skin but pull the skin down and off with the head. Locate the central bone and run a knife or your fingers between the eel flesh and the bone. Continue until the eels are completely filleted. You should have about 550 g (1¹/₄ lb) of eel fillets.

Roughly chop the eel flesh and divide into two equal piles. Blend half the fillets in a blender or food processor with all the remaining ingredients and process until smooth. Taste for seasoning and add salt and pepper as necessary. Scrape the eel butter into a clean bowl and mix in the remaining chopped eel. The pâté is now finished and can be spooned into ramekins or a pâté dish.

Alternatively we like to form a roll with cling film or aluminium foil. To do this, simply spread the cling film on a flat surface and spoon the pâté on to one end to form a large sausage shape. Roll the pâté in the cling film to make a neat cylinder and twist the ends to seal it tightly. Chill the pâté for at least 2 hours before serving. Cut into small slices and garnish with salad leaves.

ROAST FILLET OF BRILL WITH POTATO SCALES

WHEN WE FIRST STARTED COOKING FISH WITH POTATO SCALES IT SEEMED HILARIOUS AND VERY IRISH INDEED. THIS DISH HAS A BEAUTIFUL CONTRAST OF TEXTURES AND, SERVED WITH WARM LEEK VINAIGRETTE (PAGE 12), IS LIGHT YET TASTY AND SATISFYING.

SERVES 6-8

6-8 baby potatoes

salt and freshly ground white
  pepper

200 g (7 oz) unsalted butter,
  melted

6 thick brill fillets, about
  150 g (5 oz) each

plain flour for dredging

1½ tablespoons vegetable oil

Warm Leek Vinaigrette
  (page 12) to serve

Slice the potatoes as thinly as possible (about 3 mm/⅛ in) using a sharp knife or a vegetable slicer. Season them lightly with salt, cover with a damp cloth and allow to stand for 5 minutes. After this time you will notice that the potatoes have given off plenty of water and are limp and pliable. Pat the potato slices dry, then pour over them about 150 g (5 oz) of melted butter, stirring to coat the potatoes in butter. Season the brill fillets with salt and pepper, dredge lightly in flour and place on a plate. Arrange the potato slices on one side of the brill, over-lapping them slightly to give the effect of fish scales. When all the fillets are covered, chill them for at least 30 minutes to allow the potato scales to stick firmly.

Pre-heat the oven to 180°C/350°F/gas 4.

To cook the fish, heat a large, heavy-based, ovenproof frying-pan over a moderate heat. Add the oil and remaining butter and heat until the butter is foaming. Carefully place the fillets in the pan potato-side down and cook for about 3 minutes until the potatoes are beginning to brown nicely. Turn the fillets and cook for about 30 seconds to seal the other side, then turn the fish again and place the pan in the oven for 5 minutes or until the fillets are cooked and firm to the touch.

To serve, carefully turn the fillets on to warmed plates and surround with the Warm Leek Vinaigrette.

WARM LEEK VINAIGRETTE

THIS IS A DELICIOUS VINAIGRETTE THAT WILL GO WELL WITH FISH, CHICKEN OR VEGETABLE DISHES.

SERVES 6-8

3 tablespoons butter

200 ml (7 fl oz) water

450 g (1 lb) leeks, thinly sliced

salt and freshly ground white pepper

6 plum tomatoes, skinned, seeded and diced

4½ tablespoons white wine vinegar

2 teaspoons grain mustard

200 ml (7 fl oz) light olive oil

In a large pan, melt the butter and water over a high heat. Add the leeks and a little salt and cook for about 5 minutes, stirring frequently. Add the tomato and a few twists of pepper and remove from the heat.

In a small bowl, whisk together the wine vinegar, mustard, ¼ teaspoon of salt and some freshly ground pepper. Whisk in the oil, then check and adjust the seasoning to taste. Add the leek mixture to the vinaigrette and serve while still warm.

CHOCOLATE ROULADE WITH RASPBERRIES

THIS DESSERT IS LIKE A SWISS ROLL - BUT THE RICHNESS OF THE CHOCOLATE SPONGE AND THE FRESH, DELICATE FLAVOUR OF THE RASPBERRIES ELEVATES IT TO THE WINNER'S CIRCLE. EVERYONE WILL RETURN FOR SECONDS, SO BE PREPARED! YOU CAN SERVE THE ROULADE WITH EXTRA RASPBERRY SAUCE (PAGE 80) IF YOU LIKE.

SERVES 6-8

6 eggs, separated

250 g (9 oz) icing sugar, sifted

100 g (4 oz) cocoa

25 g (1 oz) cornflour

350 ml (12 fl oz) whipping cream

Pre-heat the oven to 190°C/375°F/gas 5. Grease and line a 30 x 40 cm (12 x 16 in) Swiss roll tin.

Use an electric mixture to whisk together the egg yolks with 175 g (6 oz) of icing sugar for about 3 minutes until pale in colour and very fluffy. Set aside.

In a clean bowl, whisk the egg whites until they form soft peaks. Slowly add the remaining sugar and whisk for another few minutes until glossy and firm.

50 g (2 oz) caster sugar
1 teaspoon vanilla essence
100 ml (3½ fl oz) raspberry
    jam
2 tablespoons water
225 g (8 oz) fresh
    raspberries
sprigs of fresh mint and extra
    raspberries to decorate
    (optional)

Sift together the cocoa and cornflour. Fold the cocoa mixture and egg whites alternately into the yolk mixture, making sure the mixture is well blended. Spread the mixture evenly on the prepared baking tray and bake in the pre-heated oven for about 8 minutes.

Meanwhile, whip the cream until firm. Fold in the sugar and vanilla essence and set aside. Blend together the jam and water and set aside.

Lay a clean kitchen towel on your worktop and cover with a piece of greaseproof paper. When the sponge is cooked, remove from the oven and turn out on to the greaseproof paper. As it is cooling, trim the edges of any crusty bits. Brush a thin layer of the diluted raspberry jam to cover the whole sponge. By now there should be hardly any heat left in the sponge. Quickly cover with a generous layer of the whipped cream and sprinkle generously with the fresh raspberries.

Starting at the side furthest from you, roll the sponge up lengthways finishing with the edge of the sponge underneath. Transfer to a clean baking sheet and chill for at least 1 hour to set.

To serve, cut slices at an angle and serve on individual plates, decorated, if you like, with mint and extra raspberries.

OVERLEAF

Catch of the Day, Menu 1: Smoked Eel Pâté with Fresh Herbs (page 10); Roast Fillet of Brill with Potato Scales (page 11); Chocolate Roulade with Raspberries (page 12).

RISOTTO MOLLY MALONE

MOLLY AND HER WHEELBARROW MAY NEVER HAVE MADE IT TO ITALY, BUT WE'RE SURE SHE'D APPROVE OF THIS RECIPE ANYWAY. THE TASTY JUICES THAT COME FROM THE COCKLES AND MUSSELS ARE ABSORBED INTO THE RICE, MAKING IT TASTE DELICIOUS. FEEL FREE TO USE JUST COCKLES OR MUSSELS IF YOU PREFER. ARBORIO RICE IS ONE OF THE BEST RISOTTO RICES AND IS AVAILABLE IN ALL GOOD SUPERMARKETS, OR YOU CAN USE ANY MEDIUM-GRAIN RISOTTO RICE TO ACHIEVE THE WONDERFUL CREAMY TEXTURE THAT IS ESSENTIAL FOR RISOTTO.

SERVES 4

FOR THE COCKLES AND MUSSELS

1 kg (2¼ lb) live cockles
1 kg (2¼ lb) live mussels
250 ml (8 fl oz) dry white
   wine
100 ml (3½ fl oz) water
3 tablespoons finely chopped
   onion
1 sprig of fresh thyme or ½
   teaspoon dried thyme
2 fresh parsley stalks

FOR THE RISOTTO

75 g (3 oz) unsalted butter
1 medium onion, finely
   chopped
cockle and mussel cooking
   liquid
200 g (7 oz) arborio or other
   risotto rice
salt
2 tablespoons chopped fresh
   coriander
1 tablespoon snipped fresh
   chives

Wash and scrub the cockles and mussels carefully, scraping off the beards from the mussels. Rinse them in clean water and discard any mussels that are open and do not close when tapped with a knife.

Meanwhile, bring the wine, water, onion, thyme and parsley to the boil in a large pan. Add the cockles and mussels, cover and boil vigorously for 2-3 minutes or until all cockles and mussels have opened. Discard any that remain closed. Drain into a colander with a bowl underneath to catch and reserve the cooking liquid. Make it up to 500 ml (17 fl oz) with water. As soon as they are cool enough to handle, remove them from their shells.

To cook the risotto, heat a large pan over a moderate heat. Melt 25 g (1 oz) of the butter and gently sweat the onion until soft and transparent. Meanwhile put the measured cockle/mussel liquid into a pan with a pinch of salt and bring it to the boil. Add the rice to the onion, stir well and cook gently for about 2 minutes. Add enough hot stock just to cover the rice and stir over a medium heat until most of the liquid has been absorbed into the rice. Add another good ladle of liquid and stir until this again has been absorbed. Continue in this way for about 20 minutes until the rice is cooked; it should be tender yet retain a little bite in the middle. Stir in the cooked and shelled cockles and mussels and the remaining butter and chopped herbs and allow to warm through. Serve immediately.

STEAMED HAKE WITH SLICED TOMATOES AND TARRAGON

Although we are blessed with lots of good quality hake in Ireland, it isn't one of the most popular fish. That's based more on habit than merit because fresh hake is superb. We particularly like it for this recipe because it looks so good with its bright silver skin contrasting with the pure white flesh and the ruby red tomatoes. If you cannot buy hake easily, you can substitute almost any good fresh white fish.

SERVES 4

4 hake fillets, skin on, about 175 g (6 oz) each
675 g (1½ lb) ripe tomatoes, skinned and sliced

FOR THE DRESSING

½ teaspoon salt
50 ml (2 fl oz) lemon juice
2 shallots, finely chopped
150 ml (5 fl oz) extra virgin olive oil
2 tablespoons chopped fresh tarragon

To check the hake fillets for the small bones, run your fingers lightly over the flesh to locate the bones and remove them with a pair of tweezers or small pliers. Remove any scales on the skin by scraping them off with the blunt side of a knife.

Lightly oil a steamer basket or heatproof plate and set the hake fillets into it. Steam in the steamer, or cover the plate and place over a pan of boiling water for about 6-8 minutes until tender, depending on the thickness of the fillets.

To make the dressing, dissolve the salt in the lemon juice in a small bowl. Stir in the remaining ingredients.

To serve, arrange the sliced tomatoes in a neat circle in the centre of individual warmed plates. Pour a little of the dressing over and around the tomatoes. Set the hake on top of the tomatoes and serve at once.

Roast Bananas with Waffles

BANANAS ARE A WONDERFULLY VERSATILE FRUIT THAT CAN BE USED ENDLESSLY IN DESSERTS. THEY MARRY PERFECTLY WITH CARAMEL AND RUM, AND ARE AVAILABLE ALL YEAR ROUND! A DRIZZLE OF CHOCOLATE SAUCE OR A SCOOP OF VANILLA ICE-CREAM WOULD NOT GO AMISS WITH THIS DELICIOUS DESSERT.

SERVES 4

175 g (6 oz) sugar
120 ml (4 fl oz) water
4 tablespoons Jamaican rum
2 vanilla pods
4 ripe bananas

FOR THE WAFFLES

175 ml (6 fl oz) milk
50 g (2 oz) unsalted butter
125 g (5 oz) plain flour
4 eggs
120 ml (4 fl oz) crème
   fraîche or whipping cream
grated zest of ½ lemon

Pre-heat the oven to 190°C/375°F/gas 5.

To make the waffles, grease a waffle iron and pre-heat to medium/high. If you do not have a waffle iron, you can use a griddle or heavy-based frying-pan.

Put the milk and butter in a pan and bring to the boil. As soon as it reaches boiling point, remove from heat and add all the flour at once, stirring with a wooden spoon. Place over a medium heat, stirring continuously for 1-2 minutes until it has formed a smooth mass that will not stick to the sides of the pan.

Remove from the heat and slowly beat in the eggs one at a time, either by hand or in a mixer with a dough hook. Make sure you incorporate one egg before adding the next. Lastly, pour in the crème fraîche or cream and the lemon zest and beat until well mixed.

Cook the waffles in the waffle iron following the manufactur's instructions or on the griddle or frying-pan. Cook for about 2-3 minutes each side until golden.

As they are cooking, prepare the roast bananas. First make a caramel with the sugar. Place the sugar in a heavy-based pan with half the water and let it cook over high heat until it turns a nice golden caramel colour. Remove from the heat immediately and add the rest of the water to stop the cooking. Add the rum and vanilla pods and leave to infuse off the heat.

Peel and cut the bananas diagonally into 1 cm (½ in) slices. Place in an ovenproof dish and pour over the caramel mixture. Cover with foil and bake in the pre-heated oven for about 3 minutes or until cooked through.

To serve, arrange a waffle or two (depending on size) in the centre of each warmed plate. Carefully spoon the bananas over with lots of the caramel juices. Serve at once.

CHAPTER 2

SEAFOOD BUFFET

A BUFFET IS A WONDERFUL WAY TO ENTERTAIN YOUR FRIENDS, AND SEAFOOD IS A GREAT THEME BECAUSE IT CAN INCLUDE SUCH A VARIETY OF RECIPES. THEY CAN BE SIMPLE DISHES FOR THOSE WHO LIKE THE BASIC FLAVOURS OF THEIR FOOD TO SHINE THROUGH, INTRICATE DELICACIES FOR THE ADVENTUROUS OR TRADITIONAL FAVOURITES THAT EVERYONE WILL ENJOY. THINK COLOUR, TEXTURE, CONTRAST AND HARMONY TO IMPRESS YOUR GUESTS.

MENU 1

Smoked Salmon Salad Extravaganza

....

Lobster, Mussel and White Bean Salad

....

Snow Eggs in Custard with Blackcurrant Sauce

....

MENU 2

Freshly Pickled Cod with Parsley Aïoli

....

Orzo Pasta Salad with Tomatoes and Mushrooms

....

Creamy Leek and Prawn Tart

....

Lime Tart with Papaya Sauce

....

SMOKED SALMON SALAD EXTRAVAGANZA

THIS IS A CAREFULLY COMPOSED SALAD WHICH IS A FEAST TO BEHOLD. ALL THE INGREDIENTS HAVE BEEN PUT TOGETHER TO COMPLEMENT EACH OTHER BOTH FOR TASTE AND VISUALLY. FEEL FREE TO SUBSTITUTE ANY INGREDIENTS BUT THINK ABOUT HOW THIS WILL AFFECT THE WHOLE DISH.

SERVES 6

350 g (12 oz) smoked
    salmon slices
225 g (8 oz) rocket leaves
4 ripe tomatoes, skinned and
    sliced
1 medium cucumber
1 small red onion, thinly
    sliced
4 eggs, hard-boiled
1 tablespoon snipped fresh
    chives
1 tablespoon chive flowers
12 nasturtium flowers
sprigs of fresh chervil and
    dill to garnish (optional)
Creamy Dill Dressing (page
    179) to serve

Cut away any excess dark flesh from the salmon using a small sharp knife. Arrange the smoked salmon along the middle of a large oval platter, rolling and folding it into attractive curves. Arrange the rocket leaves all around the edges of the platter. Next lay the tomato slices on both sides of the salmon but sitting on the stems of the rocket leaves to keep them in place.

Peel the cucumber, cut it in half lenthgways and scoop out the seeds with a teaspoon. Cut each half into thin slices. Lay the cucumber inside the tomato slices next to the smoked salmon. Sprinkle the onion slices over the tomatoes and cucumber. Roughly chop the egg yolks and whites separately. Sprinkle the yolks over the rocket and the whites over the smoked salmon. Sprinkle the chives and chive flowers over the salmon. Finally scatter the nasturium flowers and remaining herbs where you feel they look best. To serve, sprinkle generously with Creamy Dill Dressing.

LOBSTER, MUSSEL AND WHITE BEAN SALAD

THIS IS AN UNUSUAL SALAD INSPIRED BY FRESH LOCAL INGREDIENTS AND A FEW ITALIAN GROCERIES. ALTHOUGH IT'S ESSENTIALLY A SUMMER DISH, IT TASTES GREAT IN THE COLDER MONTHS TOO. ADAPT THE RECIPE TO WHATEVER IS AVAILABLE - PRAWNS AND MONKFISH, OR COCKLES AND SQUID TASTE WONDERFUL. FRESH, LIVE LOBSTER HAS THE BEST FLAVOUR, BUT IF YOU MUST USE COOKED LOBSTER, MAKE SURE YOU BUY IT FRESH

FROM A QUALITY SUPPLIER AND OMIT THE FIRST COOKING STAGE. IF YOU ARE SHORT OF TIME, TINS OF COOKED ITALIAN BEANS WORK VERY WELL FOR THIS RECIPE.

SERVES 6

1 x 1 kg (2¼ lb) lobster

FOR THE MUSSELS

250 ml (8 fl oz) dry white
   wine
100 ml (3½ fl oz) water
3 tablespoons finely chopped
   onion
1 sprig of fresh thyme or ½
   teaspoon dried thyme
2 fresh parsley stalks
2 kg (4½ lb) live mussels

FOR THE BEANS

225 g (8 oz) dried white
   haricot beans, soaked
   overnight in cold water
1 small onion, halved
1 small carrot
1 teaspoon salt
2 tablespoons lemon juice
6 tablespoons olive oil
½ teaspoon cracked black
   pepper

TO GARNISH

50 g (2 oz) flatleaf parsley
   leaves
4 large plum tomatoes, skinned
   and roughly chopped
salt

To cook the lobster, bring a large pan of water to a vigorous boil. Put in the lobster, cover and let it cook for about 18 minutes. Remove the lobster from the pan and stop the cooking process by plunging the lobster into a sink of cold water.

Insert a large knife into the lobster at the point where the tail and body are joined and cut towards the tail. The tail meat will now easily pull away from the shell. Break off the arms and claws and crack the shells with a heavy knife. Remove the meat, being careful to discard any pieces of shell. Slice the meat neatly and set aside.

To cook the mussels, simmer the wine, water, onion, thyme and parsley in a large pan. Meanwhile scrub the mussels and pull off the hairy beard with a sharp knife, then rinse them in cold water. Discard any that remain open and do not close when tapped with a knife. Add the mussels to the pan, cover and boil vigorously for 2 minutes or until all the mussels have opened. Discard any that remain closed. Drain the mussels into a colander with a bowl underneath to catch and reserve the broth. As soon as they are cool enough to handle, remove them from their shells.

To cook the soaked beans, drain and rinse them, then place them in a heavy-based pan and just cover with fresh water. Bring to the boil, then add the onion, carrot and salt. Cover and simmer gently for about 1 hour until the beans are tender but still hold their shape. Drain thoroughly. Toss the beans in a bowl with the lemon juice, olive oil and black pepper.

To assemble the salad, boil the mussel liquor and pour it over the beans. Add the mussels, lobster, parsley, tomatoes and toss gently. Check and adjust the seasoning to taste and serve on a large platter.

SNOW EGGS IN CUSTARD WITH BLACKCURRANT SAUCE

THESE GENTLY POACHED MERINGUE EGGS ARE LIGHT AS A FEATHER, THE PERFECT WAY TO END A MEAL. THE CUSTARD SAUCE COULD BE FLAVOURED WITH LAVENDER ESSENCE RATHER THAN VANILLA FOR AN ESPECIALLY LAVISH TOUCH. FROZEN BLACKCURRANTS ARE FINE FOR THIS DISH; LEAVE THEM TO THAW NATURALLY BEFORE USING.

SERVES 6-8

FOR THE CUSTARD

1 litre (1¾ pints) milk
1 vanilla pod, split lengthways, or 1 table-spoon vanilla essence
12 egg yolks, beaten
250 g (9 oz) caster sugar

FOR THE SNOW EGGS

6 egg whites
200 g (7 oz) caster sugar

FOR THE BLACKCURRANT SAUCE

250 g (9 oz) blackcurrants
5 tablespoons water
150 g (5 oz) caster sugar
1-2 teaspoons lemon juice
about 2 tablespoons flaked almonds to garnish

To make the custard sauce, place the milk and split vanilla pod in a heavy-based pan. Bring to the boil, then remove from the heat and allow to infuse for at least 30 minutes.

In a medium-sized bowl, whisk together the egg yolks and sugar until the sugar has dissolved. Slowly pour in the boiled milk, whisking continuously. Pour the whole mixture back into a clean pan and stir over a medium heat for about 5-10 minutes until thick. Do not allow the custard to boil. You can test that the custard is cooked by holding the spoon up and drawing a line through the custard on the spoon with your finger. If the line holds, it is ready. Place a fine sieve over a clean serving container and strain the custard into it. Allow to cool. (If using vanilla essence, rather than the pod, add at this point.)

In a large low-sided pan or non-stick frying-pan bring 2.25 litres (4 pints) of water to a simmer. Meanwhile, whisk the egg whites until they form soft peaks. Slowly add the sugar, beating gently, then whisk vigorously for 1 minute until the whites are firm and glossy.

Place a large dampened piece of greaseproof paper flat on your worktop. Fill a pastry bag fitted with a large star nozzle with the meringue mixture and pipe about 12 portions, each about 7.5 cm (3 in) in diameter and about 5 cm (2 in) high on to the dampened greaseproof paper. Carefully lift each one with a spatula and flip upside down into the simmering water. Only place as many in the pan as will fit comfortably - you don't really want them to touch each other while poaching. Poach, without allowing the water to boil, for 5 minutes. Use a slotted spoon to turn each of them over gently, then poach for a further 3 minutes until firm.

Carefully lift out the meringues and place on a clean kitchen towel to drain. Cook the remaining the meringues in the same way. Place the drained cooked snow eggs on the custard and chill in the fridge for at least 1 hour. Don't crowd the eggs as they are fragile.

While the custard and eggs are chilling, make the blackcurrant sauce. Simply place all the ingredients in a blender or food processor and process. Pass though a fine sieve and taste for flavour. Adjust with more sugar or lemon juice as necessary. Set aside.

Toast the flaked almonds by placing under a medium/hot grill or in a medium/hot oven (180°C/350°F/gas 4) until golden.

To serve, bring the serving dish out of the fridge and sprinkle on the flaked almonds, or carefully arrange a couple of snow eggs in the centre of individual soup plates and ladle some of the custard sauce around them. Decorate with toasted almonds and serve the blackcurrant sauce separately.

F R E S H L Y   P I C K L E D   C O D   W I T H   A   P A R S L E Y   A Ï O L I

POACHED FISH SERVED WITH A MINIMUM OF FUSS IS PURE AND DELICIOUS. HERE THE COD IS POACHED AND ALLOWED TO COOL IN AN AROMATIC BROTH CALLED A COURT BOUILLON. IT CAN BE SERVED STRAIGHTAWAY OR IT CAN BE CHILLED FOR A DAY OR TWO, THEN ALLOWED TO RETURN TO ROOM TEMPERATURE BEFORE SERVING. ADD AS MUCH OR AS LITTLE GARLIC TO THE AÏOLI AS YOU PREFER.

SERVES 6

6 cod steaks, about 90 g
(3 ½ oz) each

FOR THE COURT BOUILLON

50 ml (2 fl oz) white wine
vinegar
250 ml (8 fl oz) dry white
wine
500 ml (17 fl oz) water
1 small carrot, neatly sliced
1 small onion, neatly sliced
1 garlic clove, sliced
1 bay leaf
½ teaspoon coriander seeds
¼ teaspoon fennel seeds
6 white peppercorns
1 tablespoon salt

FOR THE AÏOLI

1 bunch of fresh parsley,
stalks removed
3 egg yolks
2-4 garlic cloves, finely
chopped
1½ tablespoons lemon juice
½ teaspoon salt
250 ml (8 fl oz) light olive
oil
250 ml (8 fl oz) vegetable oil

Put all the ingredients for the court bouillon in a large pan. Bring to the boil over a medium heat and simmer gently for 15-20 minutes or until the carrots are tender. Remove from the heat and allow to infuse for at least 1 hour.

To cook the cod, return the court bouillon to the boil. Add the cod steaks and simmer over a very low heat for about 2 minutes. Remove the pan from the heat and allow the cod to finish cooking as it cools down.

To make the aïoli, bring a pan of water to the boil, add the parsley leaves and blanch for 30 seconds, then drain and refresh under cold water. Pat dry with kitchen paper and chop roughly.

In a blender or food processor, combine the parsley, egg yolks, garlic, lemon juice and salt. Blend for a few seconds, then slowly add the oils in a steady stream until emulsified. Set aside.

To serve, place the cod steaks on a large serving platter with the vegetables and a little of the court bouillon. Serve the aïoli on the side.

ORZO PASTA SALAD WITH TOMATOES AND MUSHROOMS

ORZO IS A PASTA SHAPE WHICH IS JUST A LITTLE LARGER THAN LONG-GRAIN RICE. IT IS NORMALLY USED IN ITALIAN SOUPS LIKE MINESTRONE BUT IT WORKS VERY WELL FOR PASTA SALADS. IF YOU CAN'T FIND ORZO, SUBSTITUTE YOUR FAVOURITE PASTA SHAPE.

SERVES 6

225 g (8 oz) orzo pasta

275 g (10 oz) mushrooms,
  sliced or quartered

6 tablespoons finely chopped
  onion

3 tablespoons lemon juice

1/2 teaspoon salt

3 tablespoons olive oil

3 ripe tomatoes, skinned,
  seeded and diced

2 tablespoons chopped fresh
  parsley

1 tablespoon chopped fresh
  dill (optional)

salt and fresh ground black
  pepper

Bring 3 litres (5 1/4 pints) of salted water to the boil in a large pan. Add the orzo, stir well, then return the water to the boil. Cook until just *al dente*. Drain the pasta and refresh under cold running water. Allow to drain well in a colander while you prepare the mushrooms.

Bring 100 ml (3 1/2 fl oz) of water to the boil in a pan. Add the mushrooms, onion, lemon juice and salt. Cover and cook for 4 minutes. Allow to cool slightly, then add the remaining ingredients.

Combine the orzo with the mushroom mixture in an attractive serving bowl. Check the seasoning and adjust to taste with salt and pepper.

OVERLEAF

Seafood Buffet, Menu 2: Freshly Pickled Cod with a Parsley Aïoli (page 24); Orzo Pasta Salad with Tomatoes and Mushrooms (page 25); Creamy Leek and Prawn Tart (page 28); Lime Tart (page 29).

CREAMY LEEK AND PRAWN TART

REMEMBER WHEN QUICHE USED TO BE THE LATEST TRENDY FOOD? NOWADAYS IT HAS GONE OUT OF FASHION, SO WHEN WE HAVE IT ON THE MENU AT THE RESTAURANT WE CALL IT A TART. PEOPLE LOVE IT AND WE INVARIABLY RUN OUT, WHICH IS ENCOURAGING BECAUSE A GREAT DISH SHOULD NOT BE FORSAKEN JUST BECAUSE OF FICKLE FASHION. THE TART TASTES SUPERB SERVED JUST WARM WITH A SMALL SALAD.

SERVES 6

225 g (8 oz) Savoury Pastry
 (page 177)

FOR THE FILLING

25 g (1 oz) unsalted butter
100 ml (3 ½ fl oz) water
½ teaspoon salt
200 g (7 oz) leeks, thinly
 sliced
200 g (7 oz) cooked peeled
 prawns or shrimp
3 eggs
3 egg yolks
350 ml (12 fl oz) whipping
 cream
3 tablespoons tomato
 ketchup
1 tablespoon chopped fresh
 herbs such as parsley,
 tarragon, chives, basil
½ teaspoon salt
pinch of white pepper

Pre-heat the oven to 180°C/350°F/gas 4. Grease a 20 cm (8 in) flan tin.

Roll out the pastry and use it to line the prepared tin. Place in the fridge to chill for at least 20 minutes.

Cover the pastry with foil and fill with baking beans. Bake blind in the pre-heated oven for about 10 minutes until light golden brown. Remove the foil and beans and set the flan aside to cool.

Reduce the oven temperature to 150°C/300°F/gas 2.

To cook the leeks, melt the butter in a pan with the water and salt. Add the leeks and fry gently for about 4-5 minutes until just cooked. Allow the leeks to cool slightly, then squeeze out all the excess liquid. Pat the prawns dry on kitchen paper and mix them with the leeks.

In a medium bowl, whisk together the eggs and egg yolks until well blended. Add the remaining ingredients and whisk gently until the mixture is smooth. Stir in the prawn and leek mixture. Gently pour the filling into the pastry base and cook in the pre-heated oven for about 40 minutes or until the tart is completely set. Allow to cool slightly before serving.

LIME TART WITH PAPAYA SAUCE

Ⓥ

PAPAYA AND LIME MAY NOT BE THE FIRST INGREDIENTS YOU THINK OF IN RELATION TO IRISH COOKING, BUT THEY ARE A MATCH MADE IN HEAVEN! OFTEN WE SERVE THIS TART WITH A PAPAYA SORBET - IF YOU HAVE AN ICE-CREAM MACHINE YOU COULD TURN THIS PURÉE IN IT FOR PERFECT RESULTS. IF PREFERRED THIS TART COULD BE PAIRED WITH MANGO OR BLACKBERRIES.

SERVES 6-8

FOR THE LIME TART

225 g (8 oz) Shortcrust
Pastry (page 176)
8 eggs
350 g (12 oz) caster sugar
grated zest of 4 limes
250 ml (8 fl oz) whipping
cream
juices of 10-12 limes
1 egg yolk

FOR THE PAPAYA SAUCE

2 ripe papayas
juice of 3-4 limes
75 g (3 oz) sugar
100 ml (3 ½ fl oz) water

Pre-heat the oven to 190°C/375°F/gas 5. Grease a 23 cm (9 in) flan ring.

Roll out the pastry to about 3-4 mm (⅛ in) thick and use it to line the prepared flan ring. Place in the fridge to chill for 30 minutes.

Whisk the eggs, sugar and lime zest until light in colour and the mixture trails off the whisk in ribbons. Slowly whisk in the cream. Slowly add three-quarters of the lime juice. Taste the mixture and add as much of the remaining juice as you like. Set aside.

Cover the pastry with foil and fill with baking beans. Bake blind in the pre-heated oven for about 10-15 minutes. Remove the foil and beans and return the pastry to the oven for another 1-2 minutes. Remove from oven and brush the base and sides with the egg yolk to seal the pastry. Leave to cool slightly.

Reduce the oven temperature to 160°C/325°F/gas 3. Fill the pastry case with the lime mixture to just below the rim of the pastry. Bake in the pre-heated oven for about 25-30 minutes. This slower cooking ensures a smooth texture, just as one would cook a caramel custard slowly. When only the very centre jiggles slightly, the tart is cooked. Remove from oven and leave to cool.

To make the papaya sauce, halve the papayas and discard the seeds. Scoop out the flesh and place in a blender or food processor with the lime juice, sugar and water. Purée, then pass through a fine sieve. Taste to check the flavour and adjust tartness by adding a little more sugar, or sweetness by adding a little more lime juice.

To serve, place a wedge of lime tart on individual plates and ladle papaya sauce around. Serve at once.

CHAPTER 3

SUMMER BARBECUE

MOST PEOPLE GET EXCITED ABOUT THE PROSPECT OF A BARBECUE AND WITH VERY GOOD REASON - THE POSSIBILITIES ARE ENDLESS. DON'T JUST STICK TO THE OLD STAND-BYS, THINK OF THE COLOURS AND FLAVOURS OF MEDITERRANEAN AND ETHNIC FOODS, AND USE HERBS AND SPICES TO INFUSE YOUR DISHES WITH ZEST AND AROMA.

MENU 1

*Salmon Wrapped in Courgette Ribbons with
Tomato Vinaigrette*

......

Summer Barbecue Mixed Grill

......

Cos Salad Boats

......

*Lemon Cake with Nectarines and
Blackberries*

......

MENU 2

Aubergine and Olive Bruschetta

......

*King Prawn Kebabs with Sun-dried Tomato
Vinaigrette*

......

*Rice Salad with Grilled Red Onions, Peppers
and Fresh Coriander*

......

*Almond Meringue and Apricot Cream
Sandwich*

......

SALMON WRAPPED IN COURGETTE RIBBONS WITH TOMATO VINAIGRETTE

SALMON IS FANTASTIC FOR A SUMMER BARBECUE. ITS NATURAL OILS PROTECT IT FROM THE HARSH HEAT OF THE FLAMES. HOWEVER, NO AMOUNT OF OIL WILL PROTECT YOUR SALMON IF YOU OVERCOOK IT, SO BE DARING AND TRY IT A LITTLE UNDERDONE. SOAKING WOODEN SKEWERS BEFOREHAND WILL STOP THEM CHARRING WHILE ON THE BARBECUE.

SERVES 6

750 g (1½ lb) fresh salmon, skinned and boned

3 medium courgettes

salt and freshly ground black pepper

2 tablespoons light olive oil

FOR THE VINAIGRETTE

4 plum tomatoes, skinned, seeded and diced

50 g (2 oz) fresh basil leaves, chopped

100 ml (3½ fl oz) extra virgin olive oil

1 tablespoon lemon juice

¼ teaspoon salt

¼ teaspoon cracked black pepper

Pre-heat the barbecue or grill. Soak six 15 cm (6 in) wooden skewers in water for 1 hour.

Cut the salmon fillet into 2.5 cm (1 in) dice or into 24 even pieces. With a potato peeler, peel 13 cm (5 in) ribbons off the courgettes. Carefully wrap each cube of salmon with a strip of courgette. Slice and skewer each piece as it is prepared, allowing about 4 pieces of salmon per skewer. Season each one with a little salt and pepper, brush with a little olive oil and cook on the barbecue for about 5 minutes, turning occasionally, until firm and cooked.

While the salmon is cooking, mix all the ingredients for the vinaigrette in a small bowl, then divide between warmed plates. When the salmon is ready, lift the brochettes on to the plates and serve immediately.

SUMMER BARBECUE MIXED GRILL

IF YOU ARE USING THE BARBECUE, YOU MAY AS WELL COOK A FEW DIFFERENT THINGS - ESPECIALLY SINCE YOU WON'T HAVE ANY EXTRA PANS TO CLEAN. HERE WE HAVE THREE MEATS, SO WORK AHEAD AND MARINATE THE CHICKEN AND LAMB THE DAY BEFORE; THEY'LL BE ALL THE BETTER FOR IT. THE SAUSAGES CAN BE BLANCHED BEFOREHAND TOO, SO THAT THEY ONLY NEED TO BE BROWNED AND HEATED IN ORDER TO SERVE. AND THE POTATOES? WELL, OF COURSE, IN IRELAND WE BARBECUE THEM AS WELL! AS AN ALTERNATIVE TO THE COS SALAD BOATS (PAGE 34), THE SALAD OF HERBS (PAGE 169) ALSO MAKES A DELICIOUS ACCOMPANIMENT.

SERVES 6

6-12 *thick pork sausages*

FOR THE LAMB

750 g (1½ lb) boned leg of
  lamb
100 ml (3½ fl oz) light olive
  oil
1 tablespoon chopped fresh
  rosemary
2 garlic cloves, crushed
1 bay leaf

FOR THE CHICKEN

4 tablespoons vegetable oil
2 teaspoons curry powder
2 tablespoons dark soy sauce
750 g (1½ lb) boneless,
  skinless chicken thighs (or
  fillets)

Pre-heat the barbecue. Soak six wooden skewers in water for at least 30 minutes.

To blanch the sausages, bring a large pan of cold water to the boil. Add the sausages, return to the boil, then simmer for 1 minute. Drain and refresh in cold water, then chill until needed.

1.25 kg (2¹/₂ lb) small waxy
  potatoes, cooked
¹/₂ teaspoon dried oregano
¹/₂ teaspoon dried thyme
1 teaspoon chilli powder
4 tablespoons oil
salt and freshly ground black
  pepper

For the lamb, trim off any excess fat and cut into 2.5 cm (1 in) dice. Thread on to the skewers and lay in a porcelain or stainless steel dish. Simply cover with the marinade ingredients and chill for at least 12 hours.

For the chicken, mix together the marinade ingredients in a porcelain or stainless steel dish. Add the chicken thighs and rub the marinade into the chicken. Cover and chill for at least 6 hours.

Cut the potatoes in half lengthways and toss with the marinade ingredients in a large bowl. Season with salt and place them cut-side down on the barbecue. When the potatoes are well marked and nicely brown, turn them skin-side down and cook for a further 2 minutes. Place them in the oven to keep warm while you barbecue the meat.

Remove the lamb kebabs from the marinade and season with salt and pepper. Place on the barbecue and grill for about 4 minutes for medium rare or 8 minutes for well done. Remove the chicken from the marinade and season with salt and pepper. Grill on the barbecue for about 6-8 minutes or until firm. Brown the sausages quickly on the edges of the barbecue while the other meats are finishing. Serve at once.

COS SALAD BOATS

THIS IS A FUN LITTLE SALAD THAT CAN BE BUILT WITH WHATEVER IS ON HAND.

SERVES 6

12 cos salad leaves,
  preferably from the heart
2 avocados, peeled and diced
4 plum tomatoes, diced
40 g (1½ oz) alfalfa sprouts
3 eggs, hard-boiled and
  roughly chopped

FOR THE DRESSING

6 tablespoons mayonnaise
3 tablespoons water
1 teaspoon Dijon mustard
1 teaspoon chopped fresh dill
  (optional)
salt and freshly ground black
  pepper

Arrange the salad leaves on a large platter with the edges facing up so that they look like boats. Combine the avocados, tomatoes and sprouts in a bowl, then fill each of the salad leaves with this mixture. Sprinkle each one with some chopped egg.

Whisk all the dressing ingredients together in a small bowl. Check and adjust the seasoning to taste, then spoon over the salad and serve at once.

LEMON CAKE WITH NECTARINES AND BLACKBERRIES

A LIGHT, TANGY CAKE LIKE THIS ONE REVIVES THE TASTE BUDS AFTER A SUBSTANTIAL MEAL. SELECT THE BEST QUALITY FRUIT IN SEASON, OR SERVE THE CAKE ON ITS OWN OR WITH SOME WHIPPED CREAM. THE CAKE KEEPS VERY WELL WHEN COMPLETELY WRAPPED IN CLING FILM; WE FEEL IT'S EVEN TASTIER THE NEXT DAY.

SERVES 8-10

4 eggs, separated

250 g (9 oz) caster sugar

175 ml (6 fl oz) buttermilk

85 ml (3 fl oz) lemon juice

grated zest of 2 lemons

250 g (9 oz) plain flour

$1\frac{1}{4}$ teaspoons baking powder

$\frac{1}{4}$ teaspoon salt

120 g ($4\frac{1}{2}$ oz) unsalted
   butter, melted and cooled

FOR THE GLAZE

80 ml (3 fl oz) lemon juice

175 g (6 oz) icing sugar,
   sifted

FOR FRUIT DECORATION

3-4 ripe nectarines, thinly
   sliced

200 g (7 oz) fresh
   blackberries, hulled

Pre-heat the oven to 180°C/350°F/gas 4. Grease and base line a 23 cm (9 in) spring-form cake tin.

Whisk together the egg yolks and 165 g ($5\frac{1}{2}$ oz) of the sugar for 3 minutes. Slowly add the buttermilk, whisking gently, followed by the lemon juice and zest. Set aside.

In a clean bowl, whisk the egg whites until they form soft peaks. Whisking gently, pour in the remaining sugar in a slow steady stream. Whisk vigorously for 1 minute until the whites are glossy and firm.

Sift together the flour, baking powder and salt. Gently fold spoonfuls of the flour mixture then the egg whites into the egg yolk mixture until all the ingredients are well blended. Take a big serving spoon of this mixture, stir it into the cooled melted butter and mix well. Fold this butter mixture into the main bowl until everything is well mixed together. Pour into the prepared tin and cook in the pre-heated oven for 1 hour until a skewer inserted into the middle comes out clean. Remove from the oven and let the cake cool for 10 minutes, then turn out on to a wire rack to finish cooling. Using a sharp knife or skewer, poke the cake many times all over. The little holes will help the cake absorb the glaze.

To make the glaze, bring the lemon juice and icing sugar to the boil in a small pan. Boil gently for a few minutes until it thickens and has a sauce-like consistency. Gently ladle the glaze over the cake, giving the cake time to absorb the glaze so that it does not all run off the sides.

Dust the cake with a little more icing sugar and then slice it. Serve each slice on a plate and decorate with a few slices of the nectarines and a handful of berries.

AUBERGINE AND OLIVE BRUSCHETTA

BRUSCHETTA ARE GREAT FUN. IN THEIR PUREST FORM, THEY ARE SLICES OF COUNTRY BREAD TOASTED OVER OPEN COALS, THEN RUBBED WITH GARLIC WHILE STILL WARM AND DRIZZLED WITH PURE GREEN OLIVE OIL. THIS IS A SIMPLE RECIPE THAT WE'RE PARTICULARLY FOND OF, SO WHEN WE LIGHT THE BARBECUE WE ALWAYS MAKE BRUSCHETTA. TAPENADE IS A DELICIOUS OLIVE PASTE THAT IS NOW WIDELY AVAILABLE IN SUPERMARKETS.

SERVES 6

2 large aubergines, sliced 2 cm (^{3}/4 in) thick
6 x 2.5 cm (1 in) large slices of hearty country bread
150 ml (5 fl oz) olive oil
salt and freshly ground black pepper
2 garlic cloves, peeled
6 tablespoons tapenade

Pre-heat the barbecue.

With a pastry brush, brush the slices of aubergine and the bread lightly with olive oil on both sides. When the barbecue is ready, season the aubergine slices with salt and pepper and grill for 3-5 minutes on each side or until they are beautifully brown and soft right through. When the aubergines are nearly cooked, start to grill the bread slices. Don't put the bread on the hottest part of the grill or the slices will burn before they are properly toasted. Grill the bread until it is crisp and nicely brown. When the bread is cooked, rub it twice with a garlic clove, then spread it with a tablespoon of tapenade. Finish with a few slices of grilled aubergine and serve while still warm.

KING PRAWN KEBABS WITH SUN-DRIED TOMATO VINAIGRETTE

PAUL READ THE OTHER DAY IN A TOP MAGAZINE THAT SUN-DRIED TOMATOES WERE OUT OF FASHION. THE POOR OLD SUN-DRIED TOMATO - IT'S HARDLY IN AND IT'S OUT AGAIN. WHAT A LOAD OF RUBBISH! WE BELIEVE THAT IF YOU ENJOY SOMETHING - A RECIPE OR AN INGREDIENT - YOU SHOULD STICK BY IT. THIS SUN-DRIED TOMATO VINAIGRETTE IS ALSO FABULOUS WITH SALMON.

SERVES 6

900g (2 lb) or 36 large prawns, peeled and deveined

12 spring onions

1/4 teaspoon black pepper

1/2 teaspoon salt

1 tablespoon chopped fresh parsley

1 tablespoon olive oil

a few salad leaves and parsley sprigs to garnish

FOR THE VINAIGRETTE

12 sun-dried tomatoes in oil, about 100 g (4 oz), roughly chopped

200 ml (7 fl oz) light olive oil

1 teaspoon lemon juice

1/2 teaspoon chilli powder (optional)

Soak six wooden skewers in water for at least 30 minutes.

To make the vinaigrette, blend together all the ingredients in a food processor for about 1 minute or until the vinaigrette has a fairly smooth texture. Taste for seasoning because sun-dried tomatoes vary greatly in the amount of salt and flavour they contain. Adjust the seasoning to taste.

In a large bowl, toss the prawns and spring onions with the seasonings, parsley and oil. Thread the prawns and onions on to the skewers, starting with an onion followed by 6 prawns, then finishing with an onion. Grill on the barbecue for 2 minutes on each side. Serve on warmed plates with a generous spoonful of sun-dried tomato vinaigrette and a few nice salad leaves and parsley sprigs.

OVERLEAF

Summer Barbecue, Menu 2: Aubergine and Olive Bruschetta (page 36); King Prawn Kebabs with Sun-dried Tomato Vinaigrette (page 37); Rice Salad with Grilled Red Onions, Peppers and Fresh Coriander (page 40); Almond Meringue and Apricot Cream Sandwich (page 41).

RICE SALAD WITH GRILLED RED ONIONS, PEPPERS AND FRESH CORIANDER

RICE SALADS ARE GREAT IN CONCEPT BUT THEY CAN BE TERRIBLY DISAPPOINTING. THIS ONE, HOWEVER, IS PACKED FULL OF FLAVOUR SINCE THE PEPPERS AND ONIONS ARE FIRST CHARGRILLED ON THE BARBECUE AND THEN CHOPPED AND THROWN IN AT THE LAST MINUTE. IF YOU NEED TO GET EVERYTHING READY WELL IN ADVANCE, SIMPLY DICE THE PEPPERS AND ONIONS AND SAUTÉ THEM IN A LITTLE OLIVE OIL INSTEAD.

SERVES 6

300 g (11 oz) long-grain rice
6 tablespoons Standard
    Vinaigrette (page 178)
2 large red chillies, seeded
    and finely chopped
3 tablespoons chopped fresh
    coriander
salt and freshly ground black
    pepper
1 red onion
1 tablespoon olive oil
1 small yellow pepper
1 small red pepper

Pre-heat the barbecue.

Cook the rice in plenty of boiling salted water, following the directions on the packet, until just tender. Drain and refresh under cold water. Pat the rice dry in a clean cloth, then place in a serving bowl. Stir in the vinaigrette, chillies and coriander. Check and adjust the seasoning to taste.

Slice the red onion into 4 or 5 thick slices, season with a little salt and pepper and rub with olive oil. Rub the peppers with a little olive oil. When the barbecue is lit but not quite ready, put the peppers on the grill until the skins are quite charred. Now add the onions and grill for about 2 minutes on each side. Remove when they are cool enough to handle. Peel and seed the peppers and cut them into fine dice. Then dice the red onions. Add them to the rice salad and serve immediately.

ALMOND MERINGUE AND
APRICOT CREAM SANDWICH

THIS MOIST NUT MERINGUE IS A DELICIOUS FOOLPROOF RECIPE THAT COULD BE PUT WITH ANY FRUIT TO CREATE A STUNNING DESSERT. YOU COULD SUBSTITUTE GROUND HAZELNUTS, PECANS OR WALNUTS FOR THE ALMONDS, BUT BE SURE TO SKIN THEM FIRST OR THE RESULTING MERINGUE WILL BE BITTER. YOU CAN OF COURSE USE FRESH APRICOTS IF YOU JUST LIGHTLY POACH THEM.

SERVES 6

FOR THE MERINGUE

6 egg whites
185 g (6½ oz) caster sugar
215 g (7½ oz) ground
   almonds

FOR THE APRICOT CREAM

215 g (7½ oz) dried apricots
350 ml (12 fl oz) water
175 g (6 oz) caster sugar
1½ tablespoons lemon juice
250 ml (8 fl oz) whipping
   cream, softly whipped
370 g (12 oz) tinned or
   bottled apricots, drained
   and cut into 1 cm (½ in)
   dice

Pre-heat the oven to 180°C/350°F/gas 4. Line a 30 x 30 cm (12 x 12 in) baking sheet with kitchen foil.

Whisk the egg whites gently for 30 seconds, then whisk more vigorously for 1 minute until they hold soft peaks. Add 50 g (2 oz) of the sugar in a slow and steady stream, whisking vigorously until the whites are thick and glossy.

Sift the remaining sugar with the ground almonds, sprinkle the mixture over the egg whites and fold in gently until just combined. Spread the meringue in an even layer over the prepared tray so that it covers the whole tray and is even in thickness. Bake in the pre-heated oven for about 30 minutes until light golden brown and crisp but not dried out. The result should be a chewy moist meringue, not a dry crumbly one. Remove from the oven and lift carefully on to a wire rack to cool.

Place the apricots, water, sugar and lemon juice in a pan and bring to a simmer over a medium heat. Simmer gently for about 1 hour until the apricots are very soft. Remove from the heat and leave to cool slightly. Purée in a blender or food processor, then pass through a fine sieve. The resulting purée should be quite thick and intense in flavour. Fold this purée into the softly whipped cream and reserve in the fridge.

To assemble the dessert, cut 12 equal-sized rectangles from the meringue and arrange on six individual plates. Top with a generous spoonful of apricot cream and sprinkle generously with diced apricot. Dust the remaining meringue rectangles with a little icing sugar, then place on top of the apricots.

CHAPTER 4

WINTER CRAVINGS

THE SHORT DAYS OF WINTER, THE BLEAK NIGHTS AND THE RAIN THAT NEVER SEEMS TO END CONJURE UP VISIONS OF HUDDLING ROUND A BLAZING FIRE YEARNING FOR COMFORTING FOOD THAT OFFERS WARMTH AS WELL AS CONSOLATION. THESE WINTER RECIPES FIT THE BILL PERFECTLY.

<table>
<tr><td>

MENU 1

Warm Potato and Black Pudding Salad
....
Roast Goose with Traditional Sage and Onion Stuffing
....
Tangy Beetroot Purée
....
Warm Apple Charlotte
....

</td><td>

MENU 2

Smoked Salmon with Scrambled Eggs
....
Braised Lamb Shanks with Pearl Barley and Root Vegetables
....
Christmas Pudding Parfait
....

</td></tr>
</table>

WARM POTATO AND BLACK PUDDING SALAD

THIS IS A SIMPLE MEAT AND TWO VEG SALAD WHICH CAN BE SERVED AS A TASTY STARTER OR A SATISFYING LUNCH DISH. FEEL FREE TO SUBSTITUTE SAUSAGES FOR THE BLACK PUDDING IF YOU PREFER, BUT THE VERSION THAT WE GIVE HERE DOES HAVE MORE DRAMATIC COLOUR!

SERVES 6

12 small waxy salad potatoes

175 ml (6 fl oz) Standard Vinaigrette (page 178)

2 shallots, finely diced

1 tablespoon chopped fresh parsley

salt and freshly ground black pepper

1½ tablespoons vegetable oil

450 g (1 lb) black pudding, cut into 1 cm (½ in) slices

350 g (12 oz) broccoli florets

5 tablespoons meat gravy (optional)

1½ tablespoons snipped fresh chives (optional)

Place the potatoes in a small pan, cover with lightly salted water, bring to the boil and simmer over a medium high heat until tender. Drain and allow to cool slightly. Peel the potatoes and slice into 5 mm (¼ in) slices. In a small bowl, toss the potatoes in the vinaigrette with the shallots and parsley. Season with a little salt and pepper.

Heat a large frying-pan over a moderate heat, add the oil and sliced black pudding and cook for 3 minutes on each side. Add to the potatoes.

While the black pudding is cooking, bring a large pan of lightly salted water to the boil, drop in the broccoli florets and cook for 4 minutes. Drain thoroughly and add to the potatoes.

To serve, gently toss the potatoes with the broccoli and black pudding. Spoon on to warmed serving plates. Finish with a spoonful of gravy and snipped chives.

ROAST GOOSE WITH TRADITIONAL SAGE AND ONION STUFFING

THERE'S NO DOUBT THAT GOOSE IS DELICIOUS, BUT IT CAN BE DISAPPOINTING BECAUSE OF ITS LOW YIELD OF MEAT SO ALLOW ABOUT 750 G (1½ LB) PER PERSON. THIS RECIPE WILL GIVE YOU A DELICIOUS LIGHT GRAVY THAT REALLY SUITS THE RICHNESS OF THE GOOSE MEAT. THE TANGY BEETROOT PURÉE (PAGE 48) IS THE PERFECT ACCOMPANIMENT.

SERVES 6-8

3 tablespoons butter

750 g (1½ lb) onions, minced or finely chopped

30 fresh sage leaves, chopped

1 goose liver, chopped (optional)

175 g (6 oz) sausagemeat

2 egg yolks

175 g (6 oz) fresh breadcrumbs

1 x 5 kg (11 lb) goose

500 ml (17 fl oz) chicken stock or bouillon

unsalted butter, chilled and diced

salt and freshly ground black pepper

Pre-heat the oven to 220°C/425°F/gas 7.

In a large pan, melt the butter and sweat the onions over a low heat with a pinch of salt for 10 minutes. Add the sage leaves and the liver and cook for a further 2 minutes. Tip the onion mixture into a large bowl and allow to cool slightly. Mix in the sausagemeat, egg yolks and breadcrumbs and season generously with salt and pepper.

Season the goose lightly inside and out and insert the stuffing into the body cavity. Tie the legs together tightly and prick the skin with a toothpick or trussing needle to allow the fat to escape during cooking.

Lay the goose in a deep roasting tin and cook in the pre-heated oven for 30 minutes. Reduce the oven temperature to 150°C/300°C/gas 2 and cook for a further 2½ hours, basting the goose with its own fat about every 20 minutes.

Remove the goose from the oven, place on a warmed serving platter and cover with foil to rest for about 15 minutes. Pour off the fat from the roasting tray, saving all the dark roasting juices. Deglaze the roasting pan with the chicken stock or water, scraping all the caramelized juices off the bottom of the tray. Strain the juices into a clean pan and boil until reduced to about 300 ml (10 fl oz). Finally whisk in the butter and check and adjust the seasoning to taste.

To carve the goose, remove the legs and breasts first. To do this, cut the skin where the legs meet the breasts. Turn the goose on its side. Hold the drumstick with a clean cloth and pull the entire leg down towards the back. The thigh bone should pop out of its socket so that you only have to cut any awkward tendons to release the leg. Repeat with the other leg. Cut through the legs to release the drumsticks and cut each of the thighs in half, parallel to the thigh bone. This will give you six leg portions. If you need eight, utilize the wings. To release the breasts, cut along each side of the breast bone. You can then easily push the breasts away from the bone with your knife or fingers. Set the breasts on a board and cut each into six or eight pieces depending on how many servings you require. You should now have two slices of breast and one leg serving per person.

If you wish to work ahead, it is possible to do most of this in advance and simply place the portioned goose meat skin-side up on a clean oven tray; but don't slice the breast meat until you are ready to serve. Pre-heat on a low shelf underneath a hot grill with the oven door closed for about 5 minutes.

OVERLEAF

Winter Cravings, Menu 1: Warm Potato and Black Pudding Salad (page 43); Roast Goose with Traditional Sage and Onion Stuffing (page 44); Warm Apple Charlotte (page 48).

TANGY BEETROOT PURÉE

A WONDERFUL JAZZY BEETROOT RECIPE WHICH GOES VERY WELL WITH GOOSE,
DUCK, PORK OR GAME.

SERVES 6

350 g (12 oz) cooked
beetroot, sliced

1 medium onion, finely
chopped

1 garlic clove, crushed

3 tablespoons red wine
vinegar

2 tomatoes skinned, seeded
and chopped

6 tablespoons stock or
bouillon

1 teaspoon sugar

salt and freshly ground black
pepper

Pre-heat the oven to 180°C/350°F/gas 4.

Place all the ingredients in an ovenproof dish and cover tightly with foil. Cook in the pre-heated oven for 1 hour. Remove from the oven and purée in a blender or food processor until smooth. Check and adjust the seasoning to taste. Serve immediately.

WARM APPLE CHARLOTTE

WHAT MAKES A REALLY GREAT APPLE CHARLOTTE? QUALITY INGREDIENTS, OF COURSE,
FROM GOOD BREAD AND FRESH BUTTER TO TASTY BUT TART COOKING APPLES. THIS IS
ONE DESSERT THAT WILL NEVER GO OUT OF FASHION. YOU NEED TO USE METAL MOULDS
OR THE BREAD WILL NOT COLOUR PROPERLY. YOU CAN SERVE APPLE CHARLOTTE WITH
VANILLA CUSTARD SAUCE (PAGE 181), TOFFEE SAUCE (PAGE 184) OR JUST SOME
SOFTLY WHIPPED CREAM.

SERVES 6

750 g (1¾ lb) Bramley
cooking apples

300 g (11 oz) unsalted
butter, softened

Pre-heat the oven to 200°C/400°F/gas 6.

Peel and core the apples and chop them roughly. Place in a heavy-based pan with a spoonful of the butter. Add about 9 tablespoons of sugar, the lemon juice and zest and cook over medium heat until it is all soft and pulpy.

175 g (6 oz) caster sugar
grated zest and juice of 1
small lemon
about ³⁄₄ white loaf

Do not cover as you want as much moisture to evaporate off as possible, leaving a more solid mass of apple purée. Don't worry if there are some chunks, a bit of texture is nice. Adjust the flavour by adding more sugar if necessary.

Using a pastry brush, generously grease six 175 g (6 oz) metal moulds with the softened butter. Sprinkle about 4 tablespoons of sugar into the first mould, shake it about until the whole mould is well covered with sugar. Pour the excess into the next mould and do the same until you have sugared all the moulds.

Remove the crusts and slice the bread into 5 mm (¹⁄₄ in) slices. Using the pastry brush, generously coat both sides of each slice with the softened butter. Cut a round of bread to fit the bottom of each mould and then cut several slices into strips about 4 cm (1¹⁄₂ in) wide. Line the sides of each mould with the strips, slightly overlapping each to ensure no apple will escape through during the baking stage. These strips should ideally be about 5 mm (¹⁄₄ in) higher than the sides of the mould.

Now fill each mould nearly to the top with the cooled apple purée and finish by using any left-over bread pieces to cover the top. As this will be the bottom when served, it doesn't matter too much what it looks like, as long as the purée is completely covered.

Bake the charlottes in the pre-heated oven for about 10 minutes. Reduce the oven temperature to 160°C/325°F/gas 3 and continue to cook for a further 20-30 minutes. The bread should be golden and firm and the charlottes should not collapse when turned out. Remove from the oven.

To serve, simply turn out the charlottes on to individual warmed plates and serve warm but not too hot with an accompanying sauce of your choice.

SMOKED SALMON WITH SCRAMBLED EGGS

THIS DISH IS ALL ABOUT GOOD INGREDIENTS AND A LITTLE PATIENCE. THE SALMON SHOULD BE FRESH AND NOT TOO SMOKY. THE EGGS SHOULD BE FREE-RANGE WITH DEEPLY COLOURED YOLKS. AND THE PATIENCE COMES IN WHEN YOU'RE COOKING THE EGGS. THEY MUST BE STIRRED OVER A LOW HEAT UNTIL THEY JUST COME TOGETHER IN SOFT CURDS. AS A DELICIOUS ALTERNATIVE, USE PUFF PASTRY CASES INSTEAD OF THE TOASTED BAGUETTE SLICES.

SERVES 4

100 g (4 oz) smoked salmon slices
6 large free-range eggs
salt and freshly ground white pepper
25 g (1 oz) unsalted butter
2 tablespoons whipping cream
4 thick slices large baguette, cut on the angle, toasted and buttered while hot
1/2 tablespoon snipped fresh chives (optional)
1/2 tablespoon chopped fresh tarragon leaves (optional)
1/2 tablespoon chopped fresh chervil leaves (optional)

Cut the smoked salmon slices into thin strips, removing any dark pieces as you go. Taste the smoked salmon at this stage because if it is very salted you must allow for this when you season your eggs.

Break the eggs into a bowl and whisk them with a little salt and pepper until they are well mixed. Make a bain-marie by placing a large frying-pan over moderate heat and pouring in about 4 cm (1 1/2 in) of boiling water. Tip the eggs into a clean pan and place the pan in the bain-marie. Now this is where the patience is needed. Stir the eggs lazily with a wooden spoon (definitely not a whisk!), scraping the bottom of the pan as you go. The eggs will slowly form into soft, melting curds. Cook to the desired consistency then remove the pan from the bain-marie and add the butter and cream. This addition of cold ingredients will stop the cooking and will keep the eggs at the desired consistency.

Serve the eggs spooned over the toasted baguette and sprinkled generously with the smoked salmon slices and herbs. Serve at once.

Braised Lamb Shanks with Pearl Barley and Root Vegetables

This recipe is from our friend Eugene Callaghan in Gorey, County Wexford. It is typical of the tasty, hearty fare which he serves in his pub to locals and visitors alike. Shanks are meaty leg joints which are perfect for braising.

SERVES 4

4 lamb shanks

1 tablespoon vegetable oil

2 tablespoons pearl barley

300 ml (10 fl oz) lamb stock
  or water

1 fresh thyme sprig or ½
  teaspoon dried thyme

1 fresh parsley sprig

1 teaspoon salt

150 g (5 oz) carrots, roughly
  chopped

1 large leek, cut into 8 pieces

4 small potatoes, quartered

2 small onions, quartered

salt and freshly ground black
  pepper

4 heaped tablespoons parsley
  leaves, blanched and
  refreshed, to garnish

Pre-heat the oven to 160°C/325°F/gas 3.

Ask your butcher to trim off any excess fat and saw the knuckles from the shanks. Heat the oil in a large frying-pan over a high heat. Fry the lamb shanks until nicely coloured on all sides. Transfer them to a large flameproof casserole dish and add the barley, stock or water, herbs and salt. Cover tightly with foil and a lid and cook in the pre-heated oven for 1½ hours.

Remove the casserole from the oven, add the vegetables and a little more water if necessary. Season the vegetables lightly with salt and pepper, then cover the casserole and return it to the oven for a further hour.

Remove from the oven and check that the lamb is very tender and almost falling off the bone. If you think that it's not quite ready, return it to the oven for another 15 minutes.

Transfer the lamb to a warmed serving tray and cover while you finish the braised vegetables. Bring the dish back to a simmer on top of the stove, adding more water to give you a nice consistency if necessary. Add the blanched parsley leaves and check and adjust the seasoning to taste.

To serve, ladle the braised vegetables on to large warmed plates and place the shanks on top.

CHRISTMAS PUDDING PARFAIT

HAVE YOU EVER WONDERED WHAT TO DO WITH LEFT-OVER CHRISTMAS PUDDING, ESPECIALLY WHEN THERE'S ONLY A FEW PORTIONS REMAINING? THIS PARFAIT IS THE PERFECT ANSWER, AND YOU'LL BE CREATING A SIMPLE AND ELEGANT DESSERT FOR NEW YEAR'S DAY OR ANY SPECIAL YULETIDE GATHERING. WE SERVE THIS WITH BRANDIED APRICOT SAUCE (PAGE 182) BUT IT COULD BE SERVED WITH VANILLA CUSTARD SAUCE (PAGE 181) OR BRANDY BUTTER.

SERVES 4

65 g (2½ oz) white
 chocolate, chopped
175 ml (6 fl oz) double
 cream
2 tablespoons milk
¼ vanilla pod, split
3 egg yolks
1 tablespoon caster sugar
½ tablespoon brandy
175 g (6 oz) left-over
 Christmas pudding

Place the white chocolate in a heatproof bowl over a pan of hot but not boiling water and leave to melt.

Place about half the cream, the milk and the vanilla pod on to boil in another pan.

Whisk the egg yolks and the sugar together in a bowl until the sugar has dissolved. When the cream and milk has come to the boil, slowly pour it on to the yolk and sugar mixture, whisking continuously. Return to a medium heat and cook over a low heat, stirring continuously until the custard is thick enough to coat the back of a spoon. When it is ready, strain into a mixing bowl and allow to cool slightly. Add the custard to the melted chocolate, not vice versa or the resulting mixture may not be as smooth. Beat together gently for about 10 minutes. Chill for 30 minutes.

Whip the remaining cream until it forms soft peaks then fold it into the custard mixture with the brandy.

Chop the Christmas pudding into rough crumb size, by hand or using the pulse on a food processor, and fold into the parfait mixture. It's important to have chopped it into as close to crumb consistency as possible; bigger chunks aren't as nice in the finished parfait.

Line a terrine or loaf tin with cling film. Pour in the parfait, level the top and cover with cling film. Leave to set in the fridge for at least 3 hours, overnight if possible.

To serve, gently pull at the cling film surround and the parfait should release from the mould with ease. Turn out on to a flat serving plate and use a hot knife to cut a slice or two per portion, and arrange on individual plates.

CHAPTER 5

PUB GRUB

P UBS HAVE ALWAYS BEEN A FUNDAMENTAL PART OF THE
SOCIAL SCENE IN IRELAND: A PLACE TO GATHER, TO
SHARE A DRINK, EXCHANGE A TALE AND REFRESH THE
SPIRIT. WHEN IT COMES TO FOOD, HOWEVER, THE UNIDENTIFI-
ABLE LUMP OF DEFROSTED MATTER IS NO LONGER GOOD
ENOUGH. PEOPLE ARE NOW LOOKING FOR LOCAL SPECIALITIES,
FOOD THAT IS FRESH AND TASTY AND, OF COURSE, VALUE FOR
MONEY. AND WHY NOT? THE POSSIBILITIES ARE INEXHAUSTIBLE.

MENU 1

Vegetable Chowder
......

Spicy Basil Mayonnaise
......

*Ham Shanks with Horseradish Cream,
Mushrooms and Peas*
......

Derby Pie and Whipped Cream
......

MENU 2

Prawn, Avocado and Tomato Cocktail
......

*Roast Chicken Drumsticks with Parsley and
Garlic*
......

Crusty Sautéed Potatoes
......

Lime Mousse with Marinated Kiwi
......

VEGETABLE CHOWDER

WITH A PIECE OF CRUSTY BREAD AS AN ACCOMPANIMENT, A SOUP LIKE THIS IS A MEAL IN ITSELF. DON'T BE AFRAID TO LEAVE OUT A VEGETABLE IF YOU DON'T HAVE IT ON HAND, OR TO SUBSTITUTE ONE FOR ANOTHER. THIS SHOULD JUST BE A GUIDELINE TO START FROM. COURGETTES, PEAS, PUMPKIN AND FAVA BEANS ARE ALL POSSIBLE OPTIONS.

SERVES 6

200 g (7 oz) onion, finely chopped

200 g (7 oz) leeks, finely chopped

25 g (1 oz) oil or unsalted butter

100 g (4 oz) carrots, finely chopped

100 g (4 oz) celery, thinly sliced

2 garlic cloves, finely chopped

3 litres (5¼ pints) vegetable stock

1 bouquet garni (leek, bay leaf, parsley, thyme, black peppercorns)

2 teaspoons salt

300 g (11 oz) potatoes, peeled and cut into 1 cm (½ in) dice

100 g (4 oz) green beans, blanched

100 g (4 oz) cabbage, sliced and blanched

400 g (14 oz) tin chopped tomatoes

75 g (3 oz) macaroni

120 g (4½ oz) haricot beans, soaked and cooked until soft

Spicy Basil Mayonnaise (page 55) to serve

In a large heavy-based pan, sweat the onion and leeks in the oil or butter over a medium heat for about 2 minutes. Add the carrots, celery and garlic and continue to sweat for another 4 minutes, stirring occasionally, without allowing the vegetables to colour.

Add the stock, bouquet garni and salt and bring to the boil. Add the potatoes, green beans, cabbage and tomatoes. Return to the boil and simmer gently for about 15 minutes. Add the pasta and continue to simmer for about 10-15 minutes until the pasta is cooked. At the last minute, gently stir in the cooked haricot beans.

To serve, ladle into warmed soup bowls. To finish the soup, scoop in a spoonful of Spicy Basil Mayonnaise. This soup keeps well for a couple of days in the fridge.

SPICY BASIL MAYONNAISE

BY ADDING FLAVOURS AND AROMAS SUCH AS THESE, MAYONNAISE IS GIVEN A NEW LEASE OF LIFE. JUST IMAGINE THE NEW DIMENSION THIS SPICY MAYONNAISE WILL ADD TO SOUPS, SALADS OR SANDWICHES.

MAKES ABOUT 400 ML (14 FL OZ)

2 egg yolks

pinch of chilli powder

4 garlic cloves, finely chopped

4 tablespoons single cream

50 g (2 oz) chopped fresh basil leaves

275 ml (9 fl oz) light olive or vegetable oil

salt

Place the egg yolks, chilli, garlic, cream and basil in a blender or food processor. Blend or pulse for 20 seconds. Stop and push down the sides with a spatula. Blend or process again, and with the machine running, slowly and steadily pour in the oil. Check and adjust the seasoning to taste, adding salt as necessary. This mayonnaise will keep in the fridge for about 3 days.

HAM SHANKS WITH HORSERADISH CREAM, MUSHROOMS AND PEAS

THIS IS THE TYPE OF DISH THAT WILL MAKE YOU LOOK LIKE A PROFESSIONAL IN THE KITCHEN. THE HAM SHANKS CAN BE PREPARED UP TO TWO DAYS IN ADVANCE AND THE SAUCE IS A GREAT, NO-FUSS WINNER. GET READY TO IMPRESS! YOU CAN FINISH THE DISH UNDER THE GRILL IF YOU WISH. GENTLY STIR A FURTHER 120 ML (4 FL OZ) OF WHIPPED CREAM INTO THE FINISHED SAUCE, LEAVING IT IN LARGE CURDS. SERVE THE HAM ON FLAMEPROOF PLATES, SPOON THE SAUCE OVER THE HAM AND GLAZE EACH PLATE UNDER A PRE-HEATED MEDIUM GRILL FOR ABOUT 1 MINUTE. THE CURDS OF WHIPPED CREAM WILL BROWN TO GIVE A WONDERFUL GOLDEN FINISH.

SERVES 6

3 ham shanks, about 900 g
  (2 lb) each

FOR THE SAUCE

3 tablespoons unsalted butter
3 shallots or spring onions,
  finely chopped
175 g (6 oz) mushrooms,
  thinly sliced
2 tablespoons dry sherry
350 ml (12 fl oz) double
  cream
120 g (4^1/$_2$ oz) shelled peas
2-3 tablespoons creamed
  horseradish
salt and freshly ground black
  pepper
chopped fresh parsley to
  garnish

Put the shanks in a large pan of cold water. Bring to the boil, simmer for 2 minutes, then refresh under cold water. Cover again with cold water and bring to the boil. Skim off any scum which rises to the surface, cover with a lid and simmer for 2^1/$_2$-3 hours or until the meat is very tender. Transfer the shanks to a clean bowl and allow to cool. When they are cool enough to handle, remove and discard the skin. Flake the meat off the bone and cut into 2-3 cm (^{3}/$_4$-1^1/$_4$ in) chunks.

To make the sauce, heat a large pan over a moderate heat. Melt the butter and sweat the shallots or spring onions and mushrooms for 3 minutes with a little salt. Add the sherry and bring to the boil. Add the cream and peas and boil vigorously until the cream thickens.

To serve, warm the pieces of ham in a covered pan with a little of the cooking liquid or in your microwave on full power for 3 minutes. Bring the sauce to the boil and add the creamed horseradish. Do not boil again or you will spoil the flavour of the horseradish. Season to taste. Spoon the ham shanks into warmed bowls, cover generously with sauce and sprinkle with parsley.

DERBY PIE WITH WHIPPED CREAM

Ⓥ

THIS TASTY YET EASY-TO-MAKE PIE ORIGINATES IN THE DEEP SOUTHERN STATES OF AMERICA. TO US, PECANS, CHOCOLATE AND BOURBON GO TOGETHER LIKE PEAS IN A POD. IT IS BEST MADE IN A 23 CM (9 IN) PAN.

SERVES 8-10

250 g (9 oz) Shortcrust Pastry (page 176)
100 g (4 oz) pecans, chopped
4 eggs
135 g (4¾ oz) caster sugar
75 g (3 oz) plain flour
100 g (4 oz) unsalted butter, melted
2 tablespoons bourbon
1 teaspoon vanilla essence
135 g (4¾ oz) chocolate chips
whipped cream to serve

Pre-heat the oven to 180°C/350°F/gas 4.

Roll out the pastry to a thickness of about 5 mm (¼ in) and use to line a 23 cm (9 in) cast iron, ovenproof frying-pan. Chill in the fridge for at least 30 minutes.

Lightly toast the pecans by placing them on a baking sheet and putting in the pre-heated oven for about 5-10 minutes. Leave to cool.

In a large bowl, whisk together the eggs and sugar until the sugar has dissolved. Stir in the flour, butter, bourbon and vanilla essence. Fold in the chocolate chips and pecan pieces. Pour the filling into the unbaked pie crust and place in the pre-heated oven for about 40 minutes until golden.

Serve warm, with a generous dollop of whipped cream.

PRAWN, AVOCADO AND TOMATO COCKTAIL

HERE WE HAVE A VERY SIMPLE BUT PERFECT LITTLE PRAWN OR SHRIMP COCKTAIL - YOU CAN MAKE IT WITH EITHER - THAT WE LIKE TO PRESENT IN THE SAME FASHION AS THE COS SALAD BOATS (PAGE 34).

SERVES 4

350 g (12 oz) cooked
   prawns or shrimps
1 avocado, peeled and diced
8 red cherry tomatoes,
   quartered
8 yellow cherry tomatoes,
   quartered
salt and freshly ground black
   pepper
12 little green lettuce leaves
fresh coriander sprigs to
   garnish

FOR THE SAUCE

6 tablespoons natural
   yoghurt
6 tablespoons mayonnaise
2 tablespoons tomato
   ketchup
1/2 teaspoon chilli powder
2 tablespoons chopped fresh
   coriander

Make the sauce by whisking together all the ingredients in a small bowl. If you're making the sauce in advance don't add the coriander until the last moment. Without the herb, the sauce will keep for 4-5 days in the fridge.

To assemble, gently toss together the prawns or shrimp, avocado and tomatoes with half the sauce. Add a little salt and some freshly ground pepper. Now trim flat the main rib on the back of each salad leaf so that they will sit on the plate without rolling over. Put a spoonful of sauce on the middle of each plate. (This will stop the leaves from sliding around.) Fill each salad leaf with the prawn or shrimp mixture and arrange three leaves on each plate. Garnish with a sprig of coriander and serve.

ROAST CHICKEN DRUMSTICKS WITH PARSLEY AND GARLIC

DRUMSTICKS ARE A GREAT SNACK FOOD. THEY HAVE A DELICIOUS RICH TEXTURE WHICH DOESN'T DRY OUT ON RE-HEATING. THEY'RE CHEAP AND EASY TO BUY, AND KIDS LIKE THEM TOO. PAUL'S A BIG FAN, ESPECIALLY OF THIS RECIPE WHICH REMINDS HIM OF HIS FIRST TRIP TO FRANCE - IT'S BECAUSE OF THE PARSLEY AND GARLIC, OR PERSILLADE AS THE FRENCH CALL IT.

SERVES 4

12-16 chicken drumsticks
salt and freshly ground black
  pepper
1 tablespoon olive oil
4 tablespoons butter
3 garlic cloves, finely
  chopped
2 tablespoons chopped fresh
  parsley
1 tablespoon lemon juice

Season the chicken generously with salt and pepper. Heat a large heavy flameproof casserole over a moderate heat with the oil and half the butter. When the butter is foaming, add the chicken and cook until lightly browned.

Cover with a lid and cook over a gentle heat for a further 25 minutes, turning the drumsticks frequently during this period and monitoring the heat so that they fry gently. Add the remaining butter with the garlic, parsley and lemon juice and allow to infuse off the heat for a few minutes before serving.

CRUSTY SAUTÉED POTATOES

EVERYONE SEEMS TO LOVE THESE SAUTÉED POTATOES. THE SECRET IS IN THE POTATO, WHICH MUST BE FLOURY TO GIVE THE RIGHT CRUSTY TEXTURE. WE USE KERRS, PINKS, MARIS PIPER OR KING EDWARD. FOR THE RESTAURANT, WE COOK UP A LARGE BATCH OF SPUDS, THEN PEEL AND FRY THEM AS NEEDED.

SERVES 4

900 g (2 lb) floury potatoes
1 tablespoon salt
6 tablespoons vegetable oil
3 tablespoons butter

FOR THE SPICED SALT

1/2 teaspoon salt
1 teaspoon garlic salt
1 teaspoon dried thyme
1 teaspoon paprika

Put the potatoes in a large pan with the salt and cover with cold water. Bring to the boil then simmer gently for about 15-20 minutes until cooked. Drain and allow to cool. Peel off the skins with a knife and slice about 1 cm (1/2 in) thick.

Unless you have a huge frying-pan or two pans to work with, it's much better to fry these in two batches. Heat your frying-pan over a high heat. Add half the oil and butter and allow the butter to foam. Add half the potatoes and fry on each side until golden and well crusted. Mix together the spiced salt ingredients and season the potatoes with a little of the mixture. Cook for a further 1 minute, then drain on kitchen paper. If you are cooking in batches, keep them warm in the oven while you prepare the second batch, using the remaining oil and butter.

LIME MOUSSE WITH MARINATED KIWI

V

THIS LIME MOUSSE IS SUBLIME - FEATHER-LIGHT AND TASTE-BUD TANTALIZING! IT COULD EASILY BE PAIRED WITH MANGO OR PAPAYA IF PREFERRED, OR EVEN THE EXOTIC FRUIT SALAD (PAGE 112).

SERVES 4-6

2 leaves gelatine or 1½ teaspoons powdered gelatine
juice of 4 limes
4 eggs, separated
150 g (5 oz) caster sugar
finely grated zest of 2 limes
175 ml (6 fl oz) double cream
4-6 kiwi fruit
½ quantity Lime Ginger Syrup (page 112)
candied lime, cut into julienne strips
fresh mint sprigs

Soften the gelatine leaves in cold water for 5 minutes. Heat the lime juice in a small pan or in the microwave. Remove the gelatine from the cold water and dissolve in the warmed juice. Set aside.

In a bowl over a pan of simmering water, whisk together the egg yolks with 100 g (4 oz) of caster sugar for about 5 minutes until the mixture is thick and pale and trails off the whisk in ribbons. Remove from the heat and add the lime juice, dissolved gelatine and lime zest. Set the bowl over a bowl of iced water and continue to whisk gently until cold and starting to set. Whip the cream until it forms soft peaks. Whisk two of the egg whites (save the other two for another recipe) until they form soft peaks. Add the remaining sugar and whisk until glossy and firm.

Fold the whipped cream into the lime mixture. Fold in the egg whites. Taste to check the tartness, and add a little more lime juice if necessary. Pour into a serving bowl and leave to set in the fridge for at least 4 hours.

Peel the kiwi fruit and slice or cut into wedges. Ten minutes before serving, toss in Lime Ginger Syrup.

To serve, use an ice-cream scoop or large spoon to place two scoops of the lime mousse on individual plates. Using a slotted spoon, arrange some kiwi pieces around the mousse. Decorate with candied lime julienne and mint if desired.

OVERLEAF

Pub Grub, Menu 2: Prawn, Avocado and Tomato Cocktail (page 58); Roast Chicken Drumsticks with Parsley and Garlic (page 59); Crusty Sautéed Potatoes (page 60); Lime Mousse with Marinated Kiwi (page 61).

CHAPTER 6

COUNTRY FARE

To many people, country fare may suggest simple one-pot dishes, but to us it implies much more: regional specialities, family secrets passed down through the generations, and a delight in using locally available fresh produce. It takes us back to the days of self-sufficiency and living off the land.

MENU 1

Fried Pollen in Oatmeal with Tomato and Sorrel Cream

....

Grilled Whole Pollen with Sorrel Purée

....

Marinated Loin of Pork with Thyme

....

Candied Shallots

....

Pear and Walnut Upside-down Cake

....

MENU 2

Old-fashioned Salmon Mayonnaise

....

Melba Toast

....

Haunch of Venison with Red Wine, Black Pepper and Thyme

....

Celeriac Purée

....

Spiced Banana Cake with Bourbon Cream

....

FRIED POLLEN IN OATMEAL WITH TOMATO AND SORREL CREAM

POLLEN IS A FRESH WATER FISH WHICH SEEMS TO BE PECULIAR TO ONLY A FEW LAKES IN IRELAND. IT'S SOMETIMES CALLED THE FRESH WATER HERRING, BUT WE FEEL THAT IT'S CLOSER TO TROUT IN TEXTURE AND FLAVOUR. FEEL FREE TO SUBSTITUTE TROUT IN THESE RECIPES. IF YOU PREFER A HEAVIER COATING ON THE FISH, DIP THE FILLETS IN A MIXTURE OF 1 EGG BEATEN WITH 6 TABLESPOONS OF MILK BEFORE YOU ROLL THEM IN THE OATS.

SERVES 4

250 g (9 oz) rolled oats
8-12 pollen or trout fillets,
    scaled but skin on
salt and freshly ground white
    pepper
3 tablespoons vegetable oil
2 tablespoons unsalted butter

FOR THE SAUCE

1 tablespoon butter
1 cup finely shredded sorrel
    leaves
1 large plum tomato,
    skinned, seeded and diced
200 ml (7 fl oz) double
    cream

To cook the fish, first spread the oats on a large plate. Season the pollen fillets lightly with salt and pepper then roll them in the oats. Press the oats on to each fillet with your hands. Heat a large frying-pan over moderate heat and add half of the oil and butter. Wait until the butter is foaming, then add 4-6 fish fillets and fry for 2 minutes on each side. If you are cooking in batches, transfer the fish to a baking tray lined with kitchen paper and keep them warm in a low oven while you cook the rest.

To make the sauce, melt the butter in a small pan over a gentle heat. As the butter is melting, add the sorrel, tomato and a little salt and white pepper. Cook gently for about 2 minutes then add the cream. Turn up the heat a little and bring the cream to the boil. Boil gently until the cream thickens to sauce consistency, stirring occasionally. Remove from the heat, check and adjust the seasoning to taste.

To serve, lay the fillets on warmed plates and surround with a few spoonfuls of sauce.

OVERLEAF

Country Fare, Menu 1: Fried Pollen in Oatmeal with Tomato and Sorrel Cream (page 65); Marinated Loin of Pork with Thyme (page 69); Candied Shallots (page 70); Pear and Walnut Upside-down Cake (page 71).

GRILLED WHOLE POLLEN WITH SORREL PURÉE

PAUL HAS OFTEN LAMENTED THAT WE DON'T GET CERTAIN FISH IN OUR LOCAL WATERS - SUCH AS SARDINES! BUT WHEN HE TRIED CHARGRILLED POLLEN HE REALIZED THAT WE DIDN'T NEED THEM ANYWAY. THE GRILLING CRISPS THE SKIN AND HEIGHTENS THE FLAVOURS SO THAT THE FISH STANDS UP BEAUTIFULLY TO THE TANGY SORREL PURÉE. BY THE WAY, FEEL FREE TO SUBSTITUTE SARDINES! IT IS A SHAME THAT SORREL TURNS A GREEN/GREY WHEN COOKED. COOKS OFTEN TRY TO KEEP THE COLOUR BY COOKING IT LESS. THIS WORKS TO A CERTAIN EXTENT BUT WE'VE ALWAYS FOUND THAT THE FLAVOURS ARE CLEARER AND LESS ACIDIC WHEN THE SORREL LEAVES ARE PROPERLY COOKED. THIS IS AN EXCELLENT ALTERNATIVE TO THE FRIED POLLEN IN OATMEAL.

SERVES 4

8 whole pollen or trout,
    scaled and gutted
1 tablespoon vegetable oil
salt and freshly ground black
    pepper

FOR THE SORREL PURÉE

2 tablespoons unsalted butter
350 g (12 oz) sorrel leaves,
    stemmed and roughly
    chopped
150 ml (5 fl oz) whipping
    cream

Pre-heat the chargrill or grill.

Make sure that the pollen are dry or they will stick to the grill. Drizzle the fish with oil and rub it into the fish evenly. Season lightly with salt and pepper. Place on the chargrill and grill for 2-3 minutes on each side. If you're using a household grill, cover a baking sheet with lightly oiled foil and grill the fish for about 6 minutes turning once during the cooking time.

To make the sorrel purée, warm a large pan over moderate heat. Melt the butter in the pan then add the sorrel. Sweat the sorrel with a little salt for about 2 minutes. Add the cream and bring to the boil. Boil gently until the cream thickens slightly, then purée in a blender or food processor. Check and season to taste, then serve.

MARINATED LOIN OF PORK
WITH THYME

HERE WE GIVE THE PORK ROAST A LONG MARINADE SO THAT IT TAKES ON A TASTE SIMILAR TO WILD BOAR. THIS IS ONE OF THE FIRST RECIPES THAT PAUL EVER COOKED (EVEN BEFORE HE TURNED PROFESSIONAL) AND IT'S STILL ONE THAT WE COME BACK TO.

SERVES 4

1.25 kg (2½ lb) rack of pork
2 tablespoons vegetable oil
2 tablespoons unsalted
    butter, diced
salt and freshly ground black
    pepper

FOR THE MARINADE

2 garlic cloves, crushed
1 carrot, diced
1 onion, diced
100 ml (3½ fl oz) red wine
    vinegar
300 ml (10 fl oz) red wine
4 tablespoons olive oil
1 teaspoon black
    peppercorns
1½ tablespoons salt
1 teaspoon sugar
2 bay leaves
4 sprigs of fresh thyme
12 juniper berries

Pre-heat the oven to 200°C/400°F/gas 6.

Place all the marinade ingredients in a large pan and bring to the boil. Simmer for 2 minutes then allow to cool. Place the pork in a deep non-reactive (ceramic or stainless steel) container and pour the marinade over the pork. Cover with cling film and chill for 48 hours, turning every 6 hours.

After 48 hours, remove the pork from the marinade and dry with a clean cloth. Reserve the marinade. Heat a large frying-pan over high heat, add the oil and brown the pork on all sides. Transfer the pork to a roasting tray and place in the pre-heated oven for 30 minutes. Remove the roast from the oven and place the pork to rest on a large plate lightly covered with foil.

Drain any excess fat from the pan and deglaze it using 200 ml (7 fl oz) of the marinade liquid. Scrape the bottom of the pan with a wooden spoon to loosen all the delicious caramelized juices. Strain into a clean pan and boil until you have reduced the liquid by about half. Now whisk in the diced butter and check and adjust the seasoning to taste.

Carve the pork into equal portions and serve with a little sauce.

CANDIED SHALLOTS

THESE SIMPLE LITTLE BEAUTIES SEEM TO LIFT ANY ROAST MEAT INTO A HIGHER REALM.

SERVES 4

24 shallots

40 g (1½ oz) unsalted butter

1 tablespoon vegetable oil

2 tablespoons sugar

200 ml (7 fl oz) red wine or
pork marinade (page 69)

Peel the shallots carefully, leaving the root in tact to keep the shallots together. It's also nice to leave the wispy pointed ends on because they are so attractive.

Heat a large frying-pan over a moderate heat. Add the butter and oil. When the butter is foaming, add the shallots and fry gently until they turn golden in colour. Add the sugar and continue to cook for about 3 minutes until the sugar begins to caramelize. Add the red wine or marinade, cover with a lid and cook gently for 10 minutes. Remove the lid and boil off any excess liquid so that the shallots become beautifully candied.

PEAR AND WALNUT UPSIDE-DOWN CAKE

UPSIDE-DOWN CAKES LIKE THIS ARE A TRADITIONAL FAVOURITE IN THE UNITED STATES. MANY PEOPLE USE TINNED PINEAPPLE RINGS, BUT WE PREFER A FRESH FRUIT SUCH AS PEAR OR APPLE. A CARAMEL OR TOFFEE SAUCE ENHANCES THIS DESSERT, BUT SIMPLE WHIPPED CREAM MAKES IT LOVELY TOO.

SERVES 6-8

165 g (5½ oz) unsalted butter, melted
175 g (6 oz) caster sugar
175 g (6 oz) light brown sugar
4-6 ripe pears
100 g (4 oz) walnut halves

FOR SPONGE BATTER

175 g (6 oz) unsalted butter
300 g (11 oz) caster sugar
250 g (9 oz) plain flour
1½ tablespoons baking powder
½ teaspoon bicarbonate of soda
2¼ teaspoons salt
1 teaspoon cinnamon
½ teaspoon ground cloves
½ teaspoon freshly grated nutmeg
3 eggs
250 ml (8 fl oz) buttermilk
whipped cream to serve

Pre-heat the oven to 180°C/350°F/gas 4 and grease a 25 cm (10 in) round or square cake tin.

Pour the melted butter into the cake tin. Add the caster and light brown sugar and stir together with a fork until all the sugar has mixed into the butter. Set aside.

Peel, halve and core the pears. Arrange attractively, curved side down in the melted butter/sugar mixture in the cake tin. Place walnut halves in between each pear, filling in any gaps.

To make the sponge, cream together the butter and sugar until light and fluffy. Sift together all the dry ingredients. Break and lightly stir the eggs together. Add the eggs slowly to the butter and sugar mixture, making sure each addition is fully incorporated before adding more.

By hand, alternately fold in a quarter of the dry ingredients followed by one-third of the buttermilk. Continue adding the rest until all is well mixed together. Pour this batter over the pears in the cake tin and bake in the pre-heated oven for about 40 minutes or until the cake is coming away from the sides of the tin and a skewer inserted in the centre comes out clean. Remove from the oven and leave to cool for at least 10 minutes. Loosen the cake from the sides with a sharp knife and invert the cake tin on to a rimmed plate. Most of the pan juices will have been absorbed by the pears, but if there are any left, spoon them over the cake.

Serve the cake warm, sliced into individual portions, and arranged on warmed plates with whipped cream on the side.

OLD-FASHIONED SALMON MAYONNAISE

SALMON MAYONNAISE HAS BEEN SERVED IN IRISH COUNTRY HOUSES AND RESTAURANTS FOR GENERATIONS. ALTHOUGH IT KEEPS WELL IN THE FRIDGE, WE FEEL THAT IT IS AT ITS VERY BEST NEVER HAVING SEEN THE FRIDGE, AND SERVED FRESHLY MADE AT ROOM TEMPERATURE WITH LOTS OF MELBA TOAST (PAGE 73).

SERVES 4

FOR THE POACHING LIQUID

150 ml (5 fl oz) dry white
  wine
1 tablespoon vinegar
300 ml (10 fl oz) water
6 peppercorns
1 sprig of fresh parsley with
  stalk
2 teaspoons salt

450 g (1 lb) fresh salmon
  fillet, skinned
5 tablespoons mayonnaise
2 teaspoons Dijon mustard
$\frac{1}{2}$ tablespoon finely chopped
  gherkins
$\frac{1}{2}$ tablespoon chopped
  capers
$1\frac{1}{2}$ teaspoons chopped fresh
  dill
$1\frac{1}{2}$ teaspoons snipped fresh
  chives

TO GARNISH

a few salad leaves
a few sprigs of fresh dill

Combine the ingredients for the poaching liquid in a small pan and bring to the boil. Meanwhile check the salmon for bones. Cut off any brown flesh and cut into 6-8 cubes. Add the salmon to the poaching liquid and simmer for 3 minutes. Remove the pan from the heat and allow to cool.

Transfer the salmon into a medium-sized bowl. Keep the flakes large and generously sized. Fold in the remaining ingredients, garnish with salad leaves and dill, and serve at room temperature.

Melba Toast

Melba toast is a great accompaniment to almost any first course. It's also good fun to make, especially for kids. In our experience most people love Melba Toast - so make lots!

SERVES 4

4-6 slices of bread about 1 cm (½ in) thick

Trim the crusts off the bread and toast it on each side. Cut each slice in half on the diagonal. Set flat on a board and carefully cut between the two toasted sides of each slice. Set on a baking sheet cut side up until required.

Pre-heat the grill.

Finish the toast under the grill on a low shelf until crisp and warm.

HAUNCH OF VENISON WITH RED WINE, BLACK PEPPER AND THYME

THE HAUNCH IS SIMPLY THE LEG OF AN ANIMAL, AND WITH THE LOIN OF VENISON BEING SO EXPENSIVE, THE HAUNCH IS A SUPER ALTERNATIVE. ASK YOUR BUTCHER FOR A PIECE FROM THE TOP OF THE LEG WHICH WILL BE A LITTLE MORE TENDER.

SERVES 4

750 g (1¾ lb) venison leg meat, boneless
salt
2 tablespoons black pepper, cracked
1 tablespoon vegetable oil
5 tablespoons butter, cold and diced
½ tablespoon fresh thyme leaves or ½ teaspoon dried thyme
300 ml (10 fl oz) red wine
sugar
sprigs of fresh thyme to garnish

Pre-heat the oven to 180°C/350°F/gas 4.

Have your butcher trim the venison of as much sinew as possible. It would be ideal if he could 'seam out' an entire muscle which would give you a piece of meat which would be entirely sinew-free. Season the venison generously with salt. Press all but 1 teaspoon of the black pepper into the meat.

Heat a heavy ovenproof frying-pan over moderate heat. Add the oil and 2 tablespoons of butter. Allow the butter to foam, then add the venison. Brown the meat on all sides, then place in the oven. It is difficult to predict exactly how long it will take to cook because the leg meat can be many different shapes, so use these cooking times as a guideline. If you have a long thin piece it should take about 10 minutes for rare and 16 for medium to well done. A short stubby piece should take about 15 minutes for rare and 25 minutes for medium to well done. We don't recommend venison cooked more than medium well as it will tend to be very dry. When cooked, transfer the meat to a warmed plate, cover it with foil and allow it to rest while you make the sauce.

Pour any fat out of the pan and add the thyme, the remaining pepper and the red wine. Boil until only 6 tablespoons of liquid remain then remove the pan from the heat and whisk in the cold diced butter. This will mellow and thicken the sauce. Taste the sauce for seasoning and add a little sugar and salt if necessary.

Carve the venison into 1 cm (½ in) slices, adding any juices to the sauce. Arrange on warmed plates, garnish with a sprig of thyme and pour over a little sauce.

CELERIAC PURÉE

SERVES 4-6

*1 x 900 g (2 lb) celeriac,
  peeled and roughly
  chopped*
*250 g (9 oz) potatoes, peeled
  and roughly chopped*
1½ teaspoons salt
600 ml (1 pint) water
2 tablespoons butter
*300 ml (10 fl oz) whipping
  cream*
*salt and freshly ground white
  pepper*

Place the celeriac, potatoes, salt and water in a medium pan. Cover tightly and bring to the boil. Simmer very gently for about 15-20 minutes until the potatoes and celeriac are cooked. Drain into a colander, then return them to the pan with the butter and cream. Bring up to the boil, and boil until the cream thickens slightly, stirring frequently because it has a tendency to catch on the bottom. Purée in a blender or food processor until smooth. Season to taste with salt and pepper.

SPICED BANANA CAKE WITH BOURBON CREAM

THERE'S SOMETHING EXTREMELY COMFORTING ABOUT MOIST CAKES LIKE THIS. IT TASTES DELICIOUS AS A DESSERT AND YOU CAN SAVE THE REST FOR AFTERNOON TEA.

SERVES 8-10

200 g (7 oz) plain flour

175 g (6 oz) sultanas

100 g (4 oz) pecans, toasted and chopped

3/4 teaspoon cinnamon

1/2 teaspoon freshly grated nutmeg

1/4-1/2 teaspoon salt

2 teaspoons baking powder

3 ripe bananas

8 tablespoons bourbon

3 eggs

120 g (4 1/2 oz) unsalted butter

250 g (9 oz) caster sugar

400 ml (14 fl oz) whipping cream, whipped

250 ml (8 fl oz) Toffee Sauce (page 184) to serve

Pre-heat the oven to 190°C/375°F/gas 5. Grease and line a 23 cm (9 in) spring-form cake tin.

Take 2 tablespoons flour and toss the sultanas and pecans in it. This helps keep the fruit from sinking to the bottom of the batter.

Sift together all the rest of the dry ingredients except the sugar. Mash the bananas to a rough pulp with half the bourbon. Break the eggs and stir together gently. Whisk together the butter and 200 g (7 oz) of the sugar until light and fluffy. Gradually mix in the mashed banana. Slowly, mayonnaise-style, add the eggs, making sure they are fully incorporated. Fold in the dry ingredients, and finally the flour-coated fruit. Pour into the prepared cake tin and cook in the pre-heated oven for about 1 hour or until a skewer inserted in the centre comes out clean. Remove from the oven and leave to cool. Remove from the tin.

Add the remaining sugar and bourbon to the softly whipped cream.

To serve, place a slice on each plate. Dollop a spoonful of bourbon cream beside and drizzle both with Toffee Sauce.

CHAPTER 7

MEALS FROM THE MARKET

MARKET SHOPPING IS REALLY ABOUT FINDING OUT WHAT IS AVAILABLE ON THE DAY. IT'S A FUN WAY TO SHOP BECAUSE THE MARKET PLACE PERVADES ALL THE SENSES, WITH ITS SMELLS, COLOURS AND SOUNDS, WHILE THE STALL HOLDERS TRY TO LURE YOU INTO BUYING THEIR WARES.

MENU 1

Crubeens Sausage with a Mustard Crust and Sweet Peppers

....

Glazed Monkfish with Black Pepper and Ginger

....

Poached White Peaches with Raspberry Sauce

....

MENU 2

Seviche with Tomato, Lime and Fresh Coriander

....

Stir-fried Vegetable Frittata

....

Strawberry and Marscapone Torte

....

CRUBEENS SAUSAGE WITH A MUSTARD CRUST AND SWEET PEPPERS

CRUBEENS IS THE NAME USED IN IRELAND FOR PIGS' TROTTERS, AND TO MOST PEOPLE IT SOUNDS A LOT MORE APPETIZING. THIS IS A DISH THAT WE DEVELOPED TO ENCOURAGE CUSTOMERS TO TRY TROTTERS IN THE RESTAURANT AND IT WORKS VERY WELL.

SERVES 4

1 pig's trotter

1 litre (1³/4 pints) beef or chicken stock or water

1 leek, roughly chopped

1 onion, roughly chopped

1 carrot, roughly chopped

1 bouquet garni

2 red peppers

2 yellow peppers

2 tablespoons vegetable oil

200 g (7 oz) coarse sausagemeat

2¹/2 tablespoons grain mustard

100 g (4 oz) coarse breadcrumbs

2 teaspoons melted butter

1 tablespoon chopped fresh parsley

salt and freshly ground black pepper

Put the pig's trotter in a large casserole and cover with stock or water. Bring to the boil over a medium heat and skim off any scum that rises to the surface. Add the vegetables and the bouquet garni, cover and simmer slowly for about 4 hours. Remove the trotter from the liquid and allow to cool. Reserve the liquid. When cool enough to handle, flake all the meat from the bones and chop it into 1 cm (¹/2 in) dice. Reserve.

Pre-heat the oven to 200°C/400°F/gas 6.

While the trotter is cooling, rub the peppers with a tablespoon of oil and roast in the hot oven or under the grill until well blistered. Allow the peppers to cool, then peel, seed and cut into thin strips.

To make the sausage patties, simply combine the sausagemeat with the chopped crubeens. With your hands, firm it into patties about 6 cm (2¹/2 in) in diameter. Heat a heavy ovenproof frying-pan over moderate heat, add the remaining oil and fry the sausage patties for 2 minutes on one side. Turn them over and brush each one generously with the mustard. Sprinkle with breadcrumbs and top with a little melted butter. If your frying-pan fits into the oven put it in. If not transfer the patties to a roasting tray and pop them in the pre-heated oven for 10 minutes until they are firm to the touch and have a golden brown crust. Carefully transfer each one to a warmed serving plate. Add the sliced peppers to the frying-pan to deglaze all those tasty caramelized juices. Add about 6 tablespoons of the poaching stock and the parsley and bring to the boil. Season with salt and pepper and serve at once with the sausage patties.

GLAZED MONKFISH WITH BLACK PEPPER AND GINGER

THE FIRM TEXTURE AND GOOD FLAVOUR OF MONKFISH MAKES IT AN IDEAL CANDIDATE FOR THIS RECIPE. OTHER OPTIONS MIGHT BE SHARK, TURBOT OR LING, BUT WE FIND MOST PEOPLE ADORE MONKFISH. IT'S AN EXCITING ONE-PAN DISH WHERE THE FLAVOURS FROM THE EAST MEET SOME FINE FRESH PRODUCE FROM THE WEST. AN EXCELLENT ACCOMPANIMENT FOR THIS IS SOME CRISP SHREDDED CABBAGE STIR-FRIED WITH SHIITAKE MUSHROOMS.

SERVES 4

4 x 200 g (7 oz) monkfish
  fillets
salt
25 g (1 oz) black pepper,
  cracked
2 tablespoons vegetable oil
1 tablespoon butter
2 teaspoons grated fresh root
  ginger
2 teaspoons soft brown sugar
1 teaspoon black pepper,
  cracked
4 tablespoons Japanese soy
  sauce
3 tablespoons rice wine
  vinegar
100 ml (3½ fl oz) double
  cream
2 tablespoons chopped fresh
  coriander

Ask your fishmonger trim the monkfish fillets properly so that they are ready to cook.

Season each fillet lightly with salt and roll each one in the black pepper, pushing the pepper into the flesh. Heat a frying-pan over moderate heat. Add the oil and butter and heat until the butter is foaming. Add the monkfish fillets and fry for 4-5 minutes on each side..Add the ginger and fry for 30 seconds. Next add the sugar, pepper, soy sauce and rice wine vinegar and boil rapidly to reduce the liquids to a nice glaze. Roll the monkfish in the glaze and transfer to a warmed serving plate.

Add the cream and the fresh coriander to the sauce and boil until the cream thickens to sauce consistency.

POACHED WHITE PEACHES WITH RASPBERRY SAUCE

(V)

WHITE PEACHES EPITOMIZE SUMMER FRUIT. SEDUCTIVELY SCENTED, WITH SWEET JUICY FLESH, SOMETHING THIS PERFECT NEEDS LITTLE MEDDLING WITH. THE RASPBERRY SAUCE COULD EASILY BE SUBSTITUTED BY STRAWBERRY OR BLACKBERRY IF PREFERRED. TO REALLY DRESS UP THE PRESENTATION, USE TWO OR THREE FRUIT SAUCES AS WE DID ON THE TELEVISION SHOW. THE POACHING LIQUID STORES INDEFINITELY IN THE FRIDGE.

SERVES 4

500 ml (17 fl oz) water
500 g (1 lb 2 oz) caster
    sugar
1/2 bottle good quality
    sparkling wine
1/2 lemon
1 vanilla pod, split
4 ripe, unblemished white
    peaches

FOR THE RASPBERRY SAUCE
200 g (7 oz) fresh or frozen
    raspberries
100 ml (3 1/2 fl oz) water
100-150 g (4-5 oz) caster
    sugar
1 tablespoon lemon juice
sprigs of fresh mint to
    decorate

Place the water, sugar, sparkling wine, lemon and vanilla pod in a pan and bring to the boil.

With a very sharp knife, make a little cross-cut incision at the top of each peach. Gently place the peaches in the poaching liquid, cover with greaseproof paper and simmer gently for 5-10 minutes, depending upon the ripeness of the peaches. A knife will go through the flesh with no resistance when they are cooked. Remove from the heat and leave the peaches to cool in the syrup.

To make the sauce, place the raspberries, water, sugar and lemon juice in a blender or food processor, and purée. Pass through a fine sieve and taste. Adjust if necessary with more lemon or sugar, depending on the sweetness of the berries.

With a sharp knife, delicately peel the skins off the peaches. They are now ready to use or can be stored in the syrup in the fridge for up to 10 days.

To serve, ladle a generous spoonful of the raspberry sauce on to the centre of each plate. Place a drained peach in the centre, and decorate with fresh mint.

SEVICHE WITH TOMATO, LIME AND FRESH CORIANDER

SEVICHE IS THE TYPE OF DISH THAT YOU SHOULD MAKE ON MARKET DAY BECAUSE IT REQUIRES REALLY FRESH FISH. ASK YOUR FISHMONGER FOR WHATEVER IS FRESHEST. ANY FISH CAN BE USED BUT SALMON, HAKE, BRILL, SCALLOPS, MACKEREL AND HALIBUT ARE SOME OF OUR FAVOURITES.

SERVES 4

150 g (5 oz) very fresh hake, skinned

150 g (5 oz) very fresh salmon, skinned

150 ml (5 fl oz) fresh lime juice

1 teaspoon salt

freshly ground black pepper

2 ripe tomatoes, skinned, seeded and diced

2 tablespoons red onion, thinly sliced

2-4 fresh chillies, seeded and thinly sliced

1 small avocado, diced

3 tablespoons chopped fresh coriander

2 tablespoons olive oil

TO GARNISH

finely sliced salad leaves

sprigs of fresh coriander

Check the fish for any bones and cut into fine slices, or 1 cm (½ in) dice. In a ceramic or stainless steel bowl, combine the fish with the lime juice, salt and pepper. Cover and chill for 2 hours, stirring occasionally.

Remove from the fridge, add the remaining ingredients and allow to marinate for 30 minutes. Taste for seasoning, adding more salt and chilli if preferred. Serve on a 'nest' of sliced lettuce and top with a sprig of fresh coriander.

OVERLEAF

Meals from the Market, Menu 2: Seviche with Tomato, Lime and Fresh Coriander (page 81); Stir-fried Vegetable Frittata (page 84); Strawberry and Mascarpone Torte (page 85).

STIR-FRIED VEGETABLE
FRITTATA

THE WONDERFUL THING ABOUT FRITTATA ARE THEIR VERSATILITY. THEY ARE BASICALLY JUST THE ITALIAN VERSION OF A ONE-PAN OMELETTE, RATHER LIKE A SPANISH OMELETTE, AND ARE NORMALLY MADE WITH WHATEVER IS ON HAND, IN SEASON OR AT THE MARKET. YOU CAN SERVE ALSO THIS RECIPE WITH CRUSTY SAUTÉED POTATOES (PAGE 60) AND SALAD OF HERBS (PAGE 169).

SERVES 4

1 tablespoon olive oil

25 g (1 oz) unsalted butter

1 red pepper, seeded and
thinly sliced

150 g (5 oz) mushrooms,
sliced or quartered

150 g (5 oz) leeks, thinly
sliced

salt and freshly ground black
pepper

2 tablespoons water

8 eggs, beaten with ½
teaspoon salt

2 tablespoons chopped fresh
basil

4 tablespoons freshly grated
Parmesan

Pre-heat the grill to high.

Heat a large heavy frying-pan over a high heat. Add the oil and butter and allow the butter to foam. Add the pepper, mushrooms, leeks and a little salt and pepper. Stir the vegetables gently as they cook, and when the pan gets very hot again add the water. This will stop the vegetables from burning, encourage them to wilt and prevent the need for more oil.

When the vegetables are cooked to your liking, stir the eggs gently into the vegetable mixture. Add the basil and 2 tablespoons of Parmesan. Continue stirring the eggs until they begin to set, then spread the mixture evenly over the pan and sprinkle on the rest of the Parmesan.

Place the pan underneath the hot grill until the frittata is glazed and slightly puffed.

STRAWBERRY AND MASCARPONE TORTE

STRAWBERRIES AND CREAM, STRAWBERRY SHORTCAKE, BOTH ARE TRUE BLUE CLASSICS THAT ARE HARD TO BEAT. THIS TORTE STRETCHES THE COMBINATION IDEA A STEP FURTHER - THE LADY FINGERS ADD THE TEXTURE, THE MASCARPONE EGG MIXTURE IS A DELICATE LAYER OF AIRY FLUFF, AND THE STRAWBERRIES, OF COURSE, SPEAK FOR THEMSELVES! YOU CAN MAKE THE DISH IN INDIVIDUAL MOULDS OR IN ONE SOUFFLÉ DISH. AS THE RECIPE HAS SEVERAL ELEMENTS, IT IS WORTH MAKING THIS QUANTITY.

SERVES 6

900 g (2 lb) fresh
   strawberries
75 g (3 oz) caster sugar
1 tablespoon lemon juice
450 g (1 lb) Mascarpone
   cheese
150 g (5 oz) thick Pastry
   Cream (page 180)
2 tablespoons Grand
   Marnier
3 eggs, separated
6 tablespoons sugar
1 leaf gelatine, softened in
   cold water
225 g (8 oz) Savoyard
   biscuits or sponge fingers

Place 400 g (14 oz) of strawberries in a blender or food processor with the sugar and lemon juice. Blend to a smooth purée then pass through a fine sieve.

Slice the rest of the strawberries into 5 mm (1/4 in) slices and toss with a spoonful or two of the sauce, just enough to coat the slices.

In a small bowl, beat half the Mascarpone with a wooden spoon until soft. Stir in the pastry cream and half the Grand Marnier. Set aside.

Whisk the egg yolks with 3 tablespoons of sugar in a mixing bowl set over a pan of simmering water until the mixture is pale yellow, feels slightly warmer than body temperature and trails off the whisk in ribbons. Drain the gelatine from the water and whisk into the egg yolk mixture. Continue to whisk over a moderate heat until the gelatine has dissolved. Remove from the heat and beat until light and fluffy and the bowl is no longer hot.

Beat the remaining Mascarpone with a wooden spoon until soft and fold together with the gelatine, yolk and sugar mixture. Fold in the other tablespoon of Grand Marnier. Whisk the egg whites with the remaining sugar until the mixture forms soft and glossy peaks, then fold into the egg and Mascarpone mixture.

You can assemble the torte in one soufflé dish or in six 7.5 cm (3 in) soufflé moulds or pastry rings. Line the base with sponge fingers and soak them heavily with some of the strawberry sauce. Cover with a single layer of the sliced strawberries. Spoon in a 1 cm (1/2 in) thick layer of the pastry cream/Mascarpone mixture. Add another layer of sponge fingers but do not soak this layer. It will absorb enough moisture - too much will make the torte lose its shape when unmoulded. Cover with another single layer of tossed strawberries. The moulds will be just over half full. Fill to the ring with the light yolk/Mascarpone and white fluffy mixture. Place the tortes in the fridge to set for at least 2 hours.

If making in a soufflé mould, just serve it from the mould after it has been well chilled. If made in the rings, the tortes can be unmoulded. Run a hot knife around the insides of the soufflé dishes or pastry rings. Carefully tip the tortes out of the dishes or lift off the rings. Smooth out the sides if necessary with a small palette knife.

To serve, arrange in the centre of individual plates and drizzle strawberry sauce around. These tortes can keep only for a day or two in the fridge.

CHAPTER 8

FAMILY GET TOGETHER

To us, a family get together implies everyone rolling up their sleeves and getting stuck in. The kitchen is the focal point, and the preparation is a social time. For these occasions it's great to cook easy-to-serve items such as soups, roasts and the like. Be sure to make extras, for every family has at least one person who sneaks back in for the left-overs later on in the evening.

MENU 1	MENU 2

MENU 1

Chicken, Barley and Parsley Broth
....

Wheaten Bread
....

Roast Kassler with Cabbage and Potatoes
....

Chocolate Bread and Butter Pudding with Marmalade Sauce
....

MENU 2

Salmon Terrine with Sun-dried Tomato Mayonnaise
....

Turkey Ossobuco
....

Risotto with Lemon and Basil
....

Pumpkin Gingerbread
....

CHICKEN, BARLEY AND PARSLEY BROTH

THIS SOUP HAS BEEN A COMFORT FOOD TO PAUL SINCE HE WAS A WEE LAD. NUTRITIOUS AND EASY TO DIGEST, IT'S A PERFECT REMEDY FOR WHEN ONE FEELS UNDER THE WEATHER. HOWEVER, DON'T WAIT UNTIL YOU HAVE A COLD TO ENJOY IT - IT'S DELICIOUS ANY TIME! THE SOUP KEEPS WELL IN THE FRIDGE AND SOME PEOPLE THINK IT TASTES EVEN BETTER THE NEXT DAY.

SERVES 6-8

1 x 2.25 kg (5 lb) boiling
  chicken
3.9 litres (7 pints) water
400 g (14 oz) onion, finely
  chopped
250 g (9 oz) barley, soaked
  overnight in water
200 g (7 oz) carrot, grated
  (optional)
2 tablespoons salt
1 tablespoon freshly ground
  white pepper
50 g (2 oz) fresh parsley,
  finely chopped

Wash and clean the chicken and place in large pan with the cold water. Bring to the boil over a medium heat and skim off any scum that rises to the surface. Add another 300 ml (10 fl oz) of cold water (this addition helps release scum) and simmer gently for about 5 hours, skimming occasionally.

Remove the chicken and let it cool. Add the onion, soaked barley and carrot to the broth and simmer for 30 minutes. When the chicken is cool enough to handle, remove the meat from the carcass. Chop it into bite-size pieces and return it to the broth. Season with salt and pepper to taste. Just before serving the broth, add the chopped parsley.

WHEATEN BREAD

WHEATEN BREAD IS GREAT - IT HAS TEXTURE, FLAVOUR AND SO VERY MANY USES!

MAKES 1 X 900 G (2 LB) LOAF

300 g (12 oz) wholemeal
    flour, preferably course-
    textured
200 g (7 oz) plain white
    flour
15 g (½ oz) bran
1½ teaspoons bicarbonate of
    soda
pinch of salt
1 tablespoon soft brown
    sugar
600-700 ml (1-1¼ pints)
    buttermilk

Pre-heat the oven to 200°C/400°F/gas 6. Thoroughly grease a 900 g (2 lb) loaf tin.

Stir all the dry ingredients together. Stir in the buttermilk to form a nice thick dropping consistency. Pour into the prepared tin and bake in the pre-heated oven for about 1½-2 hours until the loaf sounds hollow when tapped on the base. Cool on a wire rack. If you prefer a softer crust, wrap in a slightly dampened cloth and leave to cool.

OVERLEAF

Family Get Together, Menu 1: Chicken, Barley and Parsley Broth (page 88); Roast Kassler with Cabbage and Potatoes (page 92); Chocolate Bread and Butter Pudding with Marmalade Sauce (page 93).

ROAST KASSLER WITH CABBAGE AND POTATOES

THIS IS A SIMPLE ONE-PAN DISH OF HUMBLE ORIGINS, TAKING INSPIRATION FROM THE AGE-OLD CABBAGE AND BACON RECIPES. THE SMOKED GERMAN HAM, KASSLER, PERFUMES THE CABBAGE AND POTATOES WITH ITS RICH SMOKY AROMAS. SUBSTITUTE A SMOKED BACON LOIN IF YOU CAN'T FIND KASSLER.

SERVES 6-8

1 kg (2¼ lb) potatoes,
   washed and quartered
450 g (1 lb) savoy cabbage,
   cored and roughly chopped
1 kg (2¼ lb) boned kassler
2 tablespoons unsalted butter

FOR THE SAUCE

25 g (1 oz) unsalted butter
1 tablespoon plain flour
600 ml (1 pint) chicken
   stock
50 ml (2 fl oz) Madeira or
   Port
1-3 tablespoon Dijon
   mustard
salt and freshly ground black
   pepper

Pre-heat the oven to 200°C/400°F/gas 6.

To par-boil the potatoes, place them in a large pan, cover with cold salted water and bring to the boil. Simmer for 5 minutes then drain the potatoes into a colander. This par-boiling helps to remove moisture and surface starch from the potatoes which would make them stick to the roasting tray.

Par-boil the cabbage in a large pan of lightly salted water for 2 minutes. Drain it into a colander, refresh in cold water and squeeze the cabbage dry in your hands.

Place the kassler in a large roasting tray and put in the oven. Roast it for about 10 minutes, then add the butter. When the butter has melted, add the potatoes. Roast together for 20 minutes, turning the kassler and potatoes occasionally. Push the potatoes and kassler to one side and add the cabbage. Season the potatoes and cabbage with salt. Roast for a further 10 minutes, turning all the ingredients in the smoky butter.

While the kassler is roasting, make the sauce. Melt the butter in a small pan and add the flour. Cook for 2 minutes, stirring occasionally. Take off the heat and whisk in the cold chicken stock. Whisk until smooth, then return to the heat and simmer for 20 minutes, stirring occasionally.

After a total of 40 minutes, remove the kassler from the oven. Check that the potatoes and cabbage are properly cooked and transfer them to a warmed serving platter. Slice the kassler, arrange on the cabbage and keep warm while you finish the sauce.

De-glaze the juices on the roasting tin with the Madeira and add to the sauce. Whisk in the mustard and season carefully with salt and pepper. Serve the sauce separately.

CHOCOLATE BREAD AND BUTTER PUDDING WITH MARMALADE SAUCE

CHOCOLATE ADDS ANOTHER DIMENSION TO THIS OLD FAVOURITE. IF PREFERRED, ONE
LARGE OVENPROOF DISH CAN BE USED INSTEAD OF INDIVIDUAL BOWLS.

SERVES 6-8

500 ml (17 fl oz) milk

500 ml (17 fl oz) single
   cream

grated rind of 1 orange

1 vanilla pod, split

100 g (4 oz) cocoa

1/2 loaf unsliced white bread,
   about 6 slices

8 egg yolks

2 eggs

100 g (4 oz) caster sugar

200 g (7 oz) plain chocolate,
   melted

350 g (12 oz) chunky-style
   marmalade

250 ml (8 fl oz) water

icing sugar (optional)

Place the milk, cream, orange rind and the vanilla pod
into a pan and bring to the boil. Remove from the heat,
whisk in the cocoa and leave to infuse for 30 minutes.

Pre-heat the oven to 150°C/300°F/gas 2.

Remove the crusts from the bread and cut into 5 mm
(1/4 in) slices. Cut each slice on the diagonal and place
two triangles of bread in six to eight individual ramekins.

Whisk together the egg yolks, eggs and sugar until the
sugar has dissolved. Strain the milk and cream mixture
through a fine sieve on to the eggs and sugar and whisk
together. Finally add the melted chocolate and stir well.
Ladle the mixture gently into the ramekins so as not to
disturb the bread. Place the ramekins in an oven tray and
fill it with boiling water to come one-third of the way up
the sides of the ramekins. Cover this whole bain-marie
with cling film and place in the pre-heated oven for about
40-50 minutes. The very centre of each pudding should
just shake slightly when they are ready. Remove from the
oven and remove from the bain-marie.

To make the sauce, place the marmalade and water in a
small pan and bring slowly to the boil. Stir and remove
from heat. Cover the top of each pudding with a spoonful
or two of the marmalade sauce. Alternatively, serve the
marmalade sauce on the side and simply sprinkle a little
icing sugar on to each pudding for decoration.

SALMON TERRINE WITH SUN-DRIED TOMATO MAYONNAISE

THIS IS NOT ONE OF THOSE SMOOTH TEXTURELESS TERRINES WHICH CAN BE VERY BORING AND BLAND. NO, THIS IS A BEAUTIFUL CHUNKY, FLAVOURFUL SPECIMEN THAT IS VERY VERSATILE. WE FED IT TO THE GREAT CALIFORNIAN WINE-MAKER TIM MONDAVI AND HIS CONCLUSION? 'I DON'T LIKE TERRINE, BUT I LOVE THIS ONE!'

SERVES 8

300 g (11 oz) leeks, finely
  chopped
25 g (1 oz) unsalted butter
4 tablespoons water
$1/2$ teaspoon salt

FOR THE MOUSSE

800 g ($1^3/4$ lb) fresh salmon,
  well chilled
1 egg, chilled
150 ml (5 fl oz) whipping
  cream, well chilled
$3/4$ teaspoon salt
1 tablespoon chopped fresh
  parsley
1 tablespoon snipped fresh
  chives
$1/4$ teaspoon white pepper

FOR THE SUN-DRIED
TOMATO MAYONNAISE

6 tablespoons mayonnaise
4 tablespoons Sun-dried
  Tomato Vinaigrette
  (page 37)

TO GARNISH

a few mixed salad leaves
a few sprigs of chervil

Pre-heat the oven to 160°C/325°F/gas 3. Chill the bowl and blade of a food processor for about 15 minutes. Lightly butter a 1 litre ($1^3/4$ pint) terrine dish.

Place a large pan over moderate heat and sweat the leeks with the butter, water and salt for about 5 minutes or until the leeks are lightly cooked. Drain into sieve and press with the back of a spoon to remove as much liquid as possible. Allow the leeks to cool.

To make the mousse, roughly chop about 200 g (7 oz) of the salmon and dice the remainder in 1 cm ($1/2$ in) dice. Purée the chopped salmon with the egg in the food processor until very smooth, cleaning down the sides of the bowl occasionally with a spatula. Add the cream and $1/4$ teaspoon of salt and process for 5 seconds. Wipe the sides of the bowl again and process again for 5 seconds. Transfer to a large bowl.

Add the leeks, the diced salmon and all the remaining ingredients. Mix very thoroughly, then place in the pre-pared terrine, pressing the mixture down well. Cover with a double layer of kitchen foil and stand the terrine in a large baking tin. Fill the tin with 4 cm ($1^1/2$ in) of boiling water. Place this bain-marie in the pre-heated oven and cook for 40 minutes, then remove and allow to cool. Blend together the mayonnaise and sun-dried tomato vinaigrette.

To serve, slice the terrine and place on cold plates. Garnish with a good dollop of sun-dried tomato mayonnaise and a few salad leaves and sprigs of chervil.

TURKEY OSSOBUCO

THIS IS AN IDEA WHICH PAUL NOTICED IN A COOKERY BOOK YEARS AGO AND, BEING A
BIG FAN OF THE FLAVOUR OF TURKEY LEG MEAT, HAD ALWAYS MEANT TO TRY. NOW WE
CAN'T REMEMBER THE BOOK OR FIND THE RECIPE, SO PAUL HAS DEVELOPED HIS OWN.
WE'VE BONED THE TURKEY LEGS, BUT YOU COULD SAW THE LEGS THROUGH THE BONE
INTO SECTIONS. THIS DISH RE-HEATS VERY WELL SO IT CAN BE COOKED TWO DAYS IN
ADVANCE, THEN GENTLY RE-HEATED.

SERVES 8

1.5 kg (3½ lb) turkey leg
meat, boneless, skinless
and cut in 4 cm (1½ in)
cubes

3 tablespoons plain flour

50 g (2 oz) unsalted butter

2 tablespoons oil

1 small carrot, diced

1 celery stick, diced

1 small onion, diced

1 garlic clove, finely chopped

300 ml (10 fl oz) dry white
wine

1 bay leaf

½ teaspoon dried thyme or 1
sprig of fresh thyme

450 ml (15 fl oz) meat stock
or boullion

350 g (12 oz) fresh plum
tomatoes, skinned, seeded
and diced or 1 x 400 g
(14 oz) tin of tomatoes

salt and freshly ground black
pepper

Heat a large frying-pan over moderately high heat. Roll
the turkey meat in the flour. Add the butter and oil to the
pan and allow the butter to foam. Add the turkey pieces
in one layer and fry until lightly browned on all sides. As
they brown, transfer the pieces to a flameproof casserole.
Add the diced vegetables and garlic to the frying-pan and
fry until lightly browned. Add the wine and boil until
reduced by half. Tip the wine and vegetables into the
casserole with the remaining ingredients and 1 teaspoon
of salt. Bring to the boil, then cover and simmer very
gently for 1¼ hours (or cook in a pre-heated oven at
150°C/300°F/gas 2).

When the turkey is cooked and tender, check and
season the sauce to taste and strain off any excess fat
which has floated to the surface.

RISOTTO WITH LEMON AND BASIL

THIS SIMPLE RISOTTO WAS INSPIRED BY GREMOLATA, THE DELICIOUS MIXTURE OF LEMON ZEST, PARSLEY AND GARLIC NORMALLY STREWN OVER OSSOBUCO! THE COMBINATION IS SO DELICIOUS WE DECIDED TO ADD IT TO THE RISOTTO, THEN IT CAN BE SERVED WITH SHELLFISH, CHICKEN OR WHATEVER TAKES YOUR FANCY.

SERVES 8

150 g (5 oz) unsalted butter

200 g (7 oz) onions, chopped

450 g (1 lb) arborio or other risotto rice

900 ml (1½ pints) chicken or vegetable stock, boiling hot

1 garlic clove, finely chopped

1 tablespoon grated lemon zest

2 tablespoons chopped fresh parsley

2 tablespoons chopped fresh basil

90 g (3½ oz) Parmesan, freshly grated

Melt 50 g (2 oz) of butter in a large pan over moderate heat. Add the onions and fry them gently for 5 minutes or until they are soft but have no colour. Add the rice and allow it to cook with the onions for 2 minutes, stirring well. Add enough boiling stock barely to cover the rice. Stir the rice gently until the stock has been absorbed then add another ladleful of stock and continue in this way for about 20 minutes until the rice is just cooked but has a little bite. There should be enough liquid to make the risotto creamy. Now add the remaining ingredients and stir until all the butter has been absorbed. Serve at once.

PUMPKIN GINGERBREAD

WE FIND THAT THE SWEET, SUCCULENT FLAVOUR OF PUMPKIN TENDS NOT TO BE APPRECIATED IN IRELAND. BUT IF YOU TRY THIS GINGERBREAD YOU'LL SEE HOW IT ADDS DEPTH, MOISTNESS AND A NATURAL-TASTING SWEETNESS. THE SPICES HERE COMPLEMENT ITS DELICATE FLAVOUR. IF YOU WANT TO USE FRESH PUMPKIN, SIMPLY HALVE OR QUARTER THE PUMPKIN AND SCOOP OUT THE SEEDS. PLACE THE PIECES ON A BAKING TRAY AND BAKE FOR ABOUT 1 HOUR AT 160°C/325°F/GAS 3. REMOVE FROM THE OVEN, SCRAPE ALL THE FLESH FREE AND PASS IT THROUGH A FINE SIEVE OR THROUGH A VEGETABLE MILL.

SERVES 8

250 g (9 oz) plain flour
pinch of salt
1 teaspoon bicarbonate of
　soda
2 teaspoons ground ginger
$^1/_2$ teaspoon cinnamon
$^1/_2$ teaspoon cloves
$^1/_2$ teaspoon allspice
120 ml (4 fl oz) boiling
　water
120 ml (4 fl oz) molasses
120 g ($4^1/_2$ oz) pumpkin
　purée (fresh or tinned)
185 g ($6^1/_2$ oz) granulated
　sugar
60 g ($2^1/_2$ oz) unsalted butter
1 egg
600 ml (1 pint) Vanilla
　Custard Sauce (page 181)
　made with 1 cinnamon
　stick or 1 teaspoon ground
　cinnamon

Pre-heat the oven to 180°C/350°F/gas 4. Grease a 23 cm (9 in) cake tin.

Sift together all the dry ingredients except the sugar. Mix together the boiling water and molasses. After it has cooled slightly, stir in the pumpkin purée.

Cream together the sugar and butter until light. Slowly mix in the egg and beat again until fully incorporated. Alternately fold in the dry ingredients and molasses mixture and mix thoroughly. Pour into the prepared cake tin and bake in the pre-heated oven for about 35 minutes or until a skewer inserted in the centre comes out clean. Remove from the oven and cool on a wire rack.

To make the custard, follow the custard recipe on page 181 but let the cinnamon infuse with the scalded milk for at least 30 minutes before making the custard.

To serve, slice the cake into wedges and serve each portion on a plate with a generous amount of cinnamon custard poured over the top.

CHAPTER 9

CREAM OF THE CROP

H ERE, AS THE TITLE SUGGESTS, WE'RE TALKING ABOUT THE BEST OF THE BEST. THE INGREDIENTS GIVEN IN THESE RECIPES MAY NOT ALWAYS BE IN PLENTIFUL SUPPLY, BUT IT'S WORTH SEARCHING OUT THESE TREASURED AND SOMETIMES MYSTERIOUS ITEMS. WE'VE KEPT THIS CHAPTER VEGETARIAN BECAUSE WE FEEL THAT IT REFLECTS TODAY'S TRENDS AND DEMANDS.

MENU 1

Wild Mushroom and Artichoke Tartlettes
....
Spaghetti with Baby Vegetables and Basil
....
Summer Pudding
....

MENU 2

Californian Roast Tomato and Bell Pepper Soup
....
Warm Goats' Cheese with Grilled Vegetables
....
Olive and Herb Bread
....
Lemon Curd with Fresh Strawberries
....

WILD MUSHROOM AND ARTICHOKE TARTLETTES

Ⓥ

FROM THE POINT OF VIEW OF THE PROFESSIONAL CHEF, THERE ARE FEW VEGETABLES TO
COMPARE WITH ARTICHOKES OR THE ELUSIVE WILD MUSHROOM. BOTH ARE WORTH
GETTING TO KNOW, SO TRY THIS RECIPE WITH SHIITAKE OR OYSTER MUSHROOMS, AND
SOME ARTICHOKE HEARTS, AND YOU'LL BE WELL ON YOUR WAY. INSTEAD OF FRESH
ARTICHOKES, YOU COULD USE A TIN OF GOOD QUALITY ARTICHOKES.

SERVES 4

225 g (8 oz) Savoury Pastry
   (page 177)
200 g (7 oz) wild
   mushrooms such as
   chanterelles, ceps, shiitake
   or oyster mushrooms
2 tablespoons light olive oil
2 tablespoons unsalted butter
salt and freshly ground black
   pepper
2 large artichokes or 1 x 300 g
   (11 oz) tin prepared
   artichokes hearts
juice of 1/2 lemon
1/4 garlic clove, crushed
1 tablespoon chopped fresh
   parsley

FOR THE SAUCE

100 ml (3 1/2 fl oz) whipping
   cream
100 g (4 oz) unsalted butter,
   chilled and diced
1 tablespoon lemon juice
1 tablespoon snipped fresh
   chives
1 tablespoon chopped fresh
   parsley

Grease 4 x 10 cm (4 in) tartlette tins. Roll out the pastry
to about 3 mm (1/8 in) thick and use to line the prepared
tartlette tins. Chill for at least 30 minutes in the fridge.

Pre-heat the oven to 200°C/400°F/gas 6.

Cover the pastry with greaseproof paper, fill with
baking beans and bake in the pre-heated oven for 10-15
minutes until cooked and light brown. Remove the paper
and the beans. Set aside.

Prepare the mushrooms, cleaning, cutting and trim-
ming them as necessary. Heat a large frying-pan over high
heat, add 1 tablespoon each of oil and butter and add the
mushrooms and a little salt and pepper. Fry for about 3-4
minutes until the mushrooms are cooked. Keep warm.

As you prepare the artichokes, keep them in a bowl
of water with a little lemon juice to prevent them from
discolouring; it makes no real difference to the flavour.
Carefully trim all the outside leaves with a sharp knife
until you are left with only the heart. Cut out the hairy
choke in the centre of each heart and cut each heart into
quarters. You should now have eight triangle-shaped
pieces of artichoke heart; cut each one into three slivers.

To cook, heat a frying-pan over moderate heat. Add the
remaining butter and oil, the artichokes and a little salt
and pepper. Cook over a low heat for about 10 minutes
until the artichoke slivers are soft and beginning to
brown. If you are using tinned artichokes, simply drain,
cut into manageable pieces and pan fry over high heat
until light brown. Add the mushrooms, garlic and parsley
to the artichokes. Mix together and keep warm while you
make the sauce.

To make the sauce, bring the cream to the boil in a small pan then whisk in the butter and add the lemon juice, herbs, and salt and pepper to taste. Keep warm but do not boil.

To serve, fill each tartlette shell with the artichoke and mushroom mixture. Present on warmed plates surrounded with a little sauce.

SPAGHETTI WITH BABY VEGETABLES AND BASIL

WE'VE INCLUDED THIS RECIPE HERE FOR TWO REASONS. FIRSTLY BECAUSE WE EAT IT ALL THE TIME AT HOME, AND SECONDLY TO DEMONSTRATE THE IMPORTANCE OF GOOD QUALITY INGREDIENTS. HERE WE SEE SIMPLE SPAGHETTI TRANSFORMED TO WORLD-CLASS GOURMET FODDER BY THE ADDITION OF DELICATE, TENDER VEGETABLES BURSTING WITH SEASONAL FRESHNESS. SO WHEN YOU'RE SHOPPING FOR THIS RECIPE, LEAVE YOUR LIST AT HOME AND BUY WHATEVER LOOKS GOOD AND FRESH.

SERVES 4-6

550 g (1¼ lb) spaghetti

1 tablespoon vegetable oil

50 g (2 oz) unsalted butter

50 g (2 oz) mushrooms, quartered

2 small courgettes, cut into rounds

6 red cherry tomatoes, halved

6 yellow cherry tomatoes, halved

6 baby leeks, split

200 g (7 oz) broccoli florets, cut to thumb nail size

6 asparagus spears, cut into 5 cm (2 in) lengths

6 spring onions

50 g (2 oz) fresh peas

50 g (2 oz) mangetout

50 g (2 oz) fresh basil, chopped

1 garlic clove, crushed and chopped

2 tablespoons virgin olive oil

salt and freshly ground black pepper

75 g (3 oz) Parmesan, freshly grated

Fill two large pans with about 6 litres (11 pints) of lightly salted water and bring to the boil. Add the spaghetti to one pan and boil for about 10-15 minutes until *al dente*. Meanwhile, heat a large frying-pan over a moderate heat. Add the oil and half the butter. When the butter is foaming, add the mushrooms and courgettes and cook for about 4 minutes until lightly brown and tender. Remove from the heat and add the cherry tomatoes.

While the mushrooms and courgettes are cooking, drop the remaining vegetables into the other pan, starting with vegetables that require more cooking such as leeks and broccoli. A minute later add the asparagus and spring onions, then after another minute add the peas and cook for a further 3 minutes. Drain, add to the other vegetables and keep warm.

Drain the spaghetti, then transfer it back into a warm pan. Add the basil, garlic, olive oil, remaining butter and the vegetables. Toss the spaghetti gently with the vegetables. Season with salt and pepper. Serve piping hot with the Parmesan cheese on the side.

SUMMER PUDDING

WHEN IT'S BERRY SEASON, IT'S TIME FOR SUMMER PUDDING. USE WHAT IS AVAILABLE TO YOU: STRAWBERRIES CAN BE SUBSTITUTED, LOGANBERRIES OR BLACKBERRIES AS WELL, AS LONG AS THERE'S STILL ABOUT 75 G (3 OZ) OF REDCURRANTS THE PUDDING WILL SET. WHAT COULD BE BETTER?

SERVES 4

½ loaf white bread, sliced
250 g (9 oz) blackberries
250 g (9 oz) raspberries
150 g (5 oz) redcurrants
120 g (4½ oz) caster sugar
sprigs of fresh mint to
*   decorate*
clotted, whipped or ice-
*   cream to serve (optional)*

Trim all the crusts off the bread, and use most of it to line a 600 ml (1 pint) glass bowl, covering the base and sides completely.

Place all the berries and sugar in a pan and bring to the boil. Simmer for about 3 minutes then remove from the heat. Leave to cool slightly.

Ladle the berries into the bread-lined bowl, filling to just 5 mm (¼ in) below the top, reserving any left-over juice. Cover with more bread slices and cover with a plate that fits just inside the rim of the bowl. Weigh down with a tin or two of beans on top to help compress the berries. Chill the pudding and any left-over juice in the fridge overnight.

The next day, turn the pudding out by inverting on to a rimmed plate. Pour the reserved juice over any parts of the bread that didn't take as much colour. Decorate with a mint leaf.

To serve, cut individual portions and serve with clotted cream, whipped cream or even vanilla ice-cream.

CALIFORNIAN ROAST TOMATO AND BELL PEPPER SOUP

WHEN WE LIVED IN CALIFORNIA THIS WAS ONE OF THE MOST POPULAR SOUPS AROUND. PAUL LEARNT IT FROM A CHEF WHO HAD PICKED IT UP WHILE WORKING IN THAT FAMOUS SAN FRANCISCO RESTAURANT CHEZ PANISSE. IT'S A SIMPLE SOUP WHERE EVERYTHING GOES INTO A BAKING PAN AND THEN INTO THE OVEN UNTIL TENDER, THEN IT IS PURÉED - AND THAT'S IT.

SERVES 6

1.5 kg (3¼ lb) very ripe tomatoes, halved

2 red peppers, seeded and roughly chopped

2 large onions, roughly chopped

6 garlic cloves, crushed

3 tablespoons tomato purée

3 tablespoons olive oil

1 teaspoon fresh thyme leaves

2 tablespoons fresh basil leaves

1 tablespoon fresh parsley leaves

salt and freshly ground black pepper

sugar

water or stock

TO GARNISH

6 sprigs of fresh flatleaf parsley

6 tablespoons cream

Pre-heat the oven to 200°C/400°F/gas 6.

In a fairly deep baking pan, mix all the ingredients except the herbs with 1 teaspoon of salt. Bake in the pre-heated oven for 1 hour, stirring occasionally. The skins of the tomatoes and peppers should blacken slightly.

Remove the tray from the oven and purée the soup in a blender or food processor then pass through a sieve, in batches if necessary. Put the herb leaves in the blender or food processor with a few ladles of the soup and purée for about 15 seconds. Stir it back into the soup. Correct the consistency of the soup by adding a little water or stock. Check and adjust the seasoning with salt, pepper and sugar to taste. Re-heat gently if necessary.

Serve the soup with a sprig of parsley and a tablespoon of cream in each bowl.

WARM GOATS' CHEESE WITH GRILLED VEGETABLES

WARM, GRILLED GOATS' CHEESE IS ONE OF LIFE'S SIMPLE PLEASURES. SOME SAY THAT IT IS AN ACQUIRED TASTE, BUT WE BELIEVE THEY'RE TALKING ABOUT SOMETHING OLD AND STALE, NOT THE BEAUTIFUL, TENDER, AROMATIC FRESH CHEESES THAT WE LOVE. THEY SEEM TO LEND THEMSELVES TO ANY VEGETABLE DISH, MAKING SUPERB FIRST COURSES OR SATISFYING LUNCHES. AND DON'T ALWAYS LOOK FOR A FRENCH GOAT'S CHEESE; ASK YOUR LOCAL SUPPLIER FOR IRISH OR BRITISH ONES, THEY'RE JUST AS GOOD.

SERVES 6

550 g (1¼ lb) goats' cheese
   log
2 tablespoons softened butter
a selection of grilled
   vegetables (page 110)
6 tablespoons chilli oil
cracked black pepper

Pre-heat the grill to high.

To cut the cheese neatly, take a mug of boiling water and a thin-bladed knife. Dip the knife into the water, then cut a section of cheese. Repeat until you have six neat sections. Place the cheese flat on a grill tray and spread each generously with butter. This helps the cheese brown nicely as it cooks. Cook for about 2-3 minutes or until the cheese slices are nicely browned and warmed through. With a large spatula transfer them to warmed plates. If the cheese has a rind remove it at this stage - it should simply pull off.

Surround each cheese with a selection of grilled vegetables, a little chilli oil and some cracked black pepper.

OLIVE AND HERB BREAD

THESE LITTLE ROUNDS OF BREAD ARE CHEWY AND TASTY, THE PERFECT ACCOMPANIMENT TO MANY A SOUP, SALAD OR STARTER. OF COURSE, ALTERNATIVE HERBS SUCH AS THYME OR BASIL CAN BE SUBSTITUTED; OR TRY SUN-DRIED TOMATOES INSTEAD OF OLIVES. THE BREAD ROUNDS FREEZE VERY WELL WHEN WRAPPED IN CLING FILM AND ARE HANDY TO HAVE AS STAND-BYS.

MAKES 4-6 X 15 CM (6 IN) DIAMETER ROUNDS

20 g (3/4 oz) fresh yeast
500 ml (17 fl oz) water
750 g (1 3/4 lb) strong plain flour
1 1/2 tablespoons salt
2 tablespoons olive oil
3 tablespoons finely chopped black olives
1 tablespoon finely chopped fresh parsley
1 tablespoon finely chopped fresh rosemary

Dissolve the yeast in 200 ml (7 fl oz) of warm water and leave for 10 minutes. Place the flour and salt in a mixer or food processor. Add the yeast mixture with the remaining water and the olive oil. Mix with a dough hook for several minutes. Toss in the chopped olives and herbs and mix again until the dough is shiny, elastic and smooth. Place in a greased bowl, cover with cling film and leave to rise for about 1 1/2 hours or until doubled in bulk.

Tip the risen dough on to a lightly floured surface and divide into 4-6 even portions. Taking one piece at a time, roll the dough into a ball, then roll the dough out into a 15 cm (6 in) round about 2.5 cm (1 in) thick.

Pre-heat the oven to 200°C/400°F/gas 6.

Take a razor blade or very sharp knife and score each round with about five parallel slashes, cutting right through the dough, leaving a perimeter of unslashed dough of about 2.5 cm (1 in) around the outside. Place these rounds on a floured baking tray, cover loosely with cling film and leave to rise for about 30 minutes until doubled in size.

Bake the loaves in the pre-heated oven for 25-30 minutes. Remove from oven and cool on a wire rack.

OVERLEAF

Cream of the Crop, Menu 2: Californian Roast Tomato and Bell Pepper Soup (page 103); Warm Goats' Cheese with Grilled Vegetables (page 104); Olive and Herb Bread (page 105); Lemon Curd with Fresh Strawberries (page 108).

LEMON CURD WITH FRESH STRAWBERRIES

LEMON AND STRAWBERRIES ARE SIMPLY GLORIOUS TOGETHER, BUT THIS DISH CAN EASILY BE SERVED WITH ANY OTHER BERRY OR SUMMER FRUITS SUCH AS PEACHES OR FRESH APRICOTS. YOU COULD EVEN TRY USING LIME INSTEAD OF LEMON, AND SERVE IT WITH PAPAYA OR MANGO. IF YOU LIKE A REALLY LIGHT MIXTURE, YOU CAN INCREASE THE AMOUNT OF CREAM - EVEN DOUBLE IT - BUT THIS AMOUNT GIVES A WONDERFUL TEXTURE AND TAKES THE HEAVINESS OUT OF THE CURD.

SERVES 6

2 eggs
2 egg yolks
100 g (4 oz) caster sugar
grated zest of 1-2 lemons
juice of 2 lemons (about 6
   tablespoons)
120 g (4½ oz) unsalted
   butter, chilled and diced
200 ml (7 fl oz) whipping
   cream
250 g (9 oz) fresh
   strawberries

Place the eggs, egg yolks and sugar in a heavy-based pan and whisk briskly to combine well. Add the zest and juice of the lemons, whisking again. Add the diced butter, place over a medium heat and cook, stirring continuously, for about 3 minutes without allowing the mixture to boil. If using a thermometer, the curd is ready at 160°C/325°F. Remove from the heat.

Transfer the mixture to a plastic container (it should have an airtight lid) and cover with cling film immediately. Press the cling film right against the curd and poke a slit or two with a knife to let the steam out. This will prevent a skin from forming. Leave the mixture to cool; it will thicken during the cooling period.

Whip the cream until it holds soft peaks, then fold it into the cooled mixture. Cover with the airtight lid and chill in the fridge. It will keep for about five days.

To serve, hull and halve the strawberries. Place a dollop of curd in the centre of each bowl and generously scatter strawberries all around the curd.

CHAPTER 10

SALAD MAGIC

Salads are great - healthy, easy to prepare and delicious! Is it any wonder that they are gaining so much in popularity? Whatever you do, don't be bound by the conventional lettuce - there's a whole world of salad products and condiments available, as well as, of course, your own creativity.

MENU 1

Warm Salad of Grilled Vegetables

....

Chicken Paillard on a Watercress Salad with Mustard Butter

....

Exotic Fruit Salad in Lime Ginger Syrup

....

MENU 2

Tomato and Mozzarella Salad with Basil Oil

....

Seared Beef Salad with Blue Cheese Dressing

....

Winter Soup of Poached Pears and Sun-dried Cherries with Amaretto Custard

....

WARM SALAD OF GRILLED VEGETABLES

THIS IS A SALAD THAT WE OFTEN COOK ON THE BARBECUE AT THE RESTAURANT. HERE WE'VE ADOPTED THE TECHNIQUE FOR THE HOME KITCHEN TO CREATE A MEAL IN ITSELF.

SERVES 4-6

1 red pepper
1 yellow pepper
100 ml (3½ fl oz) light olive oil
1 courgette
1 aubergine
1 red onion
1 artichoke heart, choke removed
3 small leeks, split and washed
6 large mushrooms
salt and freshly ground black pepper
a selection of salad leaves
100 ml (3½ fl oz) virgin olive oil
50 ml (2 fl oz) balsamic vinegar
100 g (4 oz) Parmesan, shaved with a peeler
1 tablespoon chopped fresh thyme
1 tablespoon chopped fresh parsley
1 tablespoon black peppercorns, cracked

To prepare the vegetables, rub the peppers with a little olive oil and roast them under a very hot grill or in a very hot oven until the skins are blackening. Peel, seed and slice each one into 6 pieces. Slice the courgette and aubergine into 1 cm (½ in) slices and drizzle lightly with light olive oil. Cut the onion and the artichoke heart into 6 wedges. Blanch the onion wedges and the leeks in a pan of boiling salted water for 2 minutes each, then drain and refresh them under cold water.

Pre-heat the grill. Arrange all the vegetables separately on grill trays and brush lightly with olive oil. Season with salt and pepper. Grill each vegetable separately until just cooked. The peppers, leeks and the artichoke only need 1-2 minutes while the mushrooms, onion, courgette and aubergine will take about 5 minutes each.

To serve, arrange the vegetables attractively on the plates and place a few mixed salad leaves in the centre of each arrangement. Drizzle with the virgin olive oil and the balsamic vinegar. Sprinkle with the Parmesan, herbs and black pepper.

CHICKEN PAILLARD ON A WATERCRESS SALAD WITH MUSTARD BUTTER

THIS IS ESSENTIALLY A MAIN COURSE LUNCH SALAD, ALTHOUGH IT WOULD WORK WELL AS A STARTER, TOO. THE DELICIOUS SAUCE IS FORMED AS THE BUTTER MELTS AND COMBINES WITH THE JUICES OF THE CHICKEN.

SERVES 4

2 tablespoons butter

2 tablespoons light vegetable oil

350 g (12 oz) cooked potato, cut into 2 cm (¾ in) dice

4 x 175 g (6 oz) chicken fillets, skinless

2 bunches of watercress

FOR THE MUSTARD BUTTER

100 g (4 oz) unsalted butter, softened

1-2 tablespoons grain mustard

few drops fresh lemon juice

salt and freshly ground white pepper

Pre-heat the grill or barbecue.

To prepare the mustard butter, beat the softened butter with 1 tablespoon of mustard in a small bowl. Taste the butter and add more mustard if desired. Add the lemon juice and season to taste with salt and pepper. Set aside.

In a large heavy frying-pan, heat half the butter and oil until it begins to colour. Sauté the potatoes until light golden and slightly crispy. Season with salt and pepper and keep warm while preparing the chicken.

Lay the chicken fillets on a cutting board. Cut into the more curved side of each, almost to the other side. Open the fillets like a book and press each one flat. Season generously with salt and pepper, brush each one with a little oil and butter and place on the highest shelf under the grill. Cook for 5 minutes on the first side, then turn over and cook for just 1 minute more. While these are cooking, prepare the watercress by picking over and washing as necessary. Dry in a salad spinner.

To serve, arrange the watercress attractively on each plate and sprinkle the sautéed potato around. Place the paillard with the nicely brown side upwards in the centre and top with a spoonful of the mustard butter.

EXOTIC FRUIT SALAD IN LIME GINGER SYRUP

A FRUIT SALAD IS ALWAYS A PLEASING WAY TO END A MEAL, AND AN EXOTIC ONE SUCH AS THIS CAN BE SUBLIME. IT CAN BE SERVED ON ITS OWN FOR A LIGHT ENDING TO A MEAL, OR YOU COULD OFFER IT WITH A FRUIT SORBET OR COCONUT ICE-CREAM. MAKE SURE YOU CHOOSE RIPE, UNBLEMISHED FRUITS THAT ARE READY FOR EATING. THE SYRUP ONLY ACCENTUATES THE FLAVOURS THAT ARE THERE - IT CAN'T ADD FLAVOUR TO FRUIT THAT IS TASTELESS OR UNDER-RIPE. IF YOU HAVE STAR FRUIT, SOME STRAWBERRIES OR EVEN A TIN OF LYCHEES, YOU CAN ADD THEM TO THE SALAD. WHATEVER FRUITS YOU ARE USING GIVE A THOUGHT TO COLOUR AND SHAPE AS YOU ARE PREPARING THEM. YOU CAN STORE THE SYRUP IN THE FRIDGE AND USE IT AGAIN AND AGAIN, SO MAKE THIS QUANTITY OF SYRUP AND JUST PREPARE ENOUGH FRUIT TO SUIT THE NUMBER YOU ARE SERVING. ALWAYS STRAIN THE SYRUP THROUGH A FINE SIEVE BEFORE STORING.

SERVES 6-8

FOR THE SYRUP

275 g (10 oz) sugar
400 ml (14 fl oz) water
40 g (1½ oz) fresh ginger
   root
pared rind of 2 limes
5 tablespoons good quality
   honey

FOR THE SALAD

1 medium pineapple
1 ripe mango
1 ripe papaya
2 kiwi fruit
candied lime zest to garnish
   (optional)

To make the syrup, place the sugar and 50 ml (2 fl oz) of water in a heavy-based pan and heat gently until the sugar has dissolved. Raise the heat the high and cook until golden caramel. Brush down the sides of the pan with a pastry brush dipped in water a couple of times as it is boiling. This helps reduce the chance of the caramel crystallizing. Remove from the heat and slowly add the rest of the water. Be careful as this may spit and splutter. Return to allow heat just until all the caramel has dissolved. Take off the heat and add the peeled ginger, lime rind and honey. Set aside to infuse for at least 30 minutes.

Meanwhile prepare the various exotic fruits. Peel and core the pineapple, and slice into attractive pieces. Do the same with the mango. Peel and seed the papaya and peel the kiwi fruits before slicing or cutting up. Place all the fruit in a bowl.

About 10 minutes before serving, strain the syrup through a fine sieve and pour it over the fruit. If using more delicate items such as strawberries, only marinate them for 1-2 minutes as they will start to go very mushy if left too long.

To serve, ladle individual portions of the exotic fruits into glass bowls with enough of the syrup. Decorate with candied lime zest if desired.

TOMATO AND MOZZARELLA SALAD WITH BASIL OIL

(V)

IT MAY SEEM A LITTLE ODD HAVING A TOMATO AND MOZZARELLA SALAD IN A GOURMET IRELAND BOOK. BUT WE DO HAVE THE TOMATOES AND THE BASIL, AND WE OCCASIONALLY GET A SUPERB ENGLISH MOZZARELLA FROM NEALS YARD IN LONDON. THIS IS A SALAD THAT IS HUGELY ENJOYED AT THE RESTAURANT.

SERVES 4

2-3 ripe red tomatoes
2-3 ripe yellow tomatoes
400 g (14 oz) fresh
   Mozzarella in brine
salt and cracked black
   pepper
6 large fresh basil leaves,
   finely shredded

FOR THE BASIL OIL
MAKES 200 ML (7 FL OZ)

175 g (6 oz) basil leaves
175 ml (6 fl oz) olive oil
1 garlic clove, crushed
$1/4$ teaspoon salt

Blanch the tomatoes by placing them in boiling water for 12 seconds. Refresh immediately under cold water. This process loosens the skin and they should peel very easily. Cut each tomato in half, and then each half into quarters. Drain the Mozzarella from the brine. Cut the Mozzarella in the same way as the tomatoes so that you have pieces which are a similar size and shape. Season the tomatoes lightly with salt. Arrange the tomato and Mozzarella pieces on large plates in almost a checkerboard fashion but leaving spaces in between each piece.

To make the basil oil, simply process all the ingredients together in a blender or food processor or a mortar and pestle until you have a fairly smooth mixture.

To finish each plate, drip a little of the basil oil from a spoon into the spaces left between the tomatoes and cheese so that you have a beautiful contrast of colours. Sprinkle each plate with some cracked black pepper and shredded basil.

OVERLEAF

Salad Magic, Menu 2: Tomato and Mozzarella Salad with Basil Oil (page 113); Seared Beef Salad with Blue Cheese Dressing (page 116); Winter Soup of Poached Pears and Sun-dried Cherries with Amaretto Custard (page 117).

SEARED BEEF SALAD WITH BLUE CHEESE DRESSING

IN OUR OPINION BEEF AND BLUE CHEESE GO TOGETHER FAMOUSLY. THE RIGHT TOUCH IS REQUIRED, THOUGH, AND THE SEARING OF THE BEEF IN THIS RECIPE LIGHTENS ITS FLAVOUR SO THAT IT STANDS UP TO THE CHEESE. THIS WOULD MAKE A GREAT QUICK LUNCH OR A BUFFET DISH AS EVERYTHING CAN BE PREPARED EVEN A DAY AHEAD AND THEN ASSEMBLED AT THE LAST MINUTE.

SERVES 4

350 g (12 oz) beef fillet, trimmed and in one piece

1 tablespoon olive oil

1/2 teaspoon salt

2 teaspoons black pepper, cracked

FOR THE CELERY

3 celery sticks, sliced diagonally 1 cm (1/2 in) thick

150 ml (5 fl oz) water

3 tablespoons olive oil

1/4 teaspoon salt

1/2 teaspoon black pepper, cracked

FOR THE DRESSING

50 g (2 oz) blue cheese, crumbled, such as Cashel Blue, Stilton, Roquefort

150 ml (5 fl oz) Standard Vinaigrette (page 178)

TO SERVE AND GARNISH

mixed salad leaves

1 tablespoon snipped fresh chives

a few fresh chervil leaves

Make sure that the beef fillet is trimmed and free of sinew and fat. Cut it in half lengthways so that you have two longish flat pieces. Season these with olive oil, salt and pepper.

Heat a cast iron frying-pan over a high heat until very hot. Add the beef and cook for 2 minutes on each side for rare or 5 for medium well. This is quite a smoky process but the final result makes it worthwhile. When cooked, transfer the beef to a plate and allow to cool.

To cook the celery, place it in a small pan with the other ingredients. Cover tightly with foil and simmer for 4 minutes. Remove the pan from the heat and allow the celery to cook in the liquid.

To make the dressing, simply whisk the crumbled cheese with the vinaigrette in a small bowl.

To serve, slice the beef into about 12 slices. Arrange the beef slices on cold plates with a little celery in between each. Place the salad leaves in the centre and spoon on a little dressing. Finish with the snipped chives and a few chervil leaves.

Winter Soup of Poached Pears and Sun-dried Cherries with Amaretto Custard

Warm soups of custard and fruit may not spring to mind immediately for most people as a dessert option, but once tried, forever appreciated. You can use tinned pears if you don't have time to poach fresh fruit (page 80). You'll find that the sun-dried cherries are available in most delicatessens but if you can't find them try sultanas or dried blueberries.

An amaretti biscuit or two would be a great accompaniment to serve with this, but isn't essential. They are Italian biscuits with a bitter almond flavour and are available in most large supermarkets or delicatessens.

SERVES 4

500 ml (17 fl oz) milk
½ vanilla pod, split or ½
   teaspoon vanilla essence
75 g (3 oz) ground almonds
6 large egg yolks
100 g (4 oz) caster sugar
50 ml (2 fl oz) amaretto
   liqueur
4 poached pears (page 80,
   omitting the wine)
60 g sun-dried cherries,
   soaked in boiling water
   until cooled
40 g (1½ oz) flaked
   almonds, toasted
amaretti biscuits to serve

Place the milk, vanilla pod and ground almonds in a pan over a moderate to high heat and bring to the boil. Remove from the heat and leave to infuse for about 20 minutes.

Whisk egg yolks and sugar together in a bowl until lightened in colour and the sugar has dissolved. Whisking continuously, slowly pour the milk into the egg yolk and sugar mixture and whisk together. Pour this mixture back into the pan and stir over a low heat until the mixture has thickened enough to coat the back of the spoon and will hold if you run your finger along the middle of the back of the spoon. When it has reached the desired thickness, strain the custard through a fine mesh sieve. Remove the vanilla pod and scrape the seeds into the custard. Stir in the liqueur. Place the custard in a heated thermos flask to keep it nice and warm for serving.

Lay the poached pears on a tray lined with kitchen paper to drain off the excess liquid. Halve, core and slice the pears into fine wedges or slices. Set aside.

To serve, arrange the pear slices and plumped up cherries in soup plates and pour the warm amaretto custard sauce over and around them. Decorate with a sprinkle of toasted flaked almonds and, if desired, some amaretti biscuits on the side.

DINNER FOR TWO FOR £10

WE ALL AT ONE TIME OR ANOTHER HAVE OCCASIONS WHEN IT IS NECESSARY TO COUNT EVERY PENNY AND WORK OUT THE COST OF EVERYTHING. BUT DON'T TAKE IT SO BAD, LOOK AT IT AS A CHANCE TO BE CREATIVE. GOOD FOOD DOESN'T ALWAYS HAVE TO BE EXPENSIVE. WITH A LITTLE THOUGHT, AND PERHAPS A LITTLE MORE LABOUR, IT'S POSSIBLE TO COME UP WITH SOME MENUS THAT ARE REAL WINNERS.

MENU 1

Crispy Fried Cod with Lentils and Vinegar
....
Breast of Turkey with Leeks, Mushrooms and Sliced Potatoes
....
Stuffed Baked Pear
....

MENU 2

Tomato Salad with Shallots, Balsamic Vinegar and Thyme
....
Skate with Chilli and Basil Cream
....
Spiced Roast Cabbage
....
Peach Crumble with Raspberry Cream
....

CRISPY FRIED COD WITH LENTILS AND VINEGAR

THIS RECIPE TAKES ITS INSPIRATION FROM DEEP-FRIED COD AND MUSHY PEAS. THIS
VERSION IS VERY MUCH LIGHTER AND PRETTIER BUT HAS ALL THE FLAVOURS.

SERVES 2

2 cod fillets x 100 g (4 oz)

4 tablespoons whipping cream

1 egg white

1 teaspoon chopped fresh
  parsley

FOR THE LENTILS

50 g (2 oz) puy lentils

350 ml (12 fl oz) stock

1/2 teaspoon salt

1 tablespoon finely diced
  onion

1 tablespoon finely diced
  carrot

1 tablespoon finely diced leek

1 tablespoon finely diced
  celery

1 tablespoon finely diced
  potato

3 tablespoons sherry vinegar

50 g (2 oz) unsalted butter,
  chilled and diced

FOR THE SPICED FLOUR

4 tablespoons plain flour

2 teaspoons baking powder

1/2 teaspoon cayenne pepper

1/2 teaspoon ground thyme

1/2 teaspoon white pepper

1/2 teaspoon garlic powder

1/2 teaspoon salt

vegetable oil for deep-frying

To cook the lentils, first rinse in plenty of cold water then put into a small pan with the stock and salt. Bring to the boil and simmer for 10 minutes. Add the vegetable dice and cook for a further 10-15 minutes or until the vegetables and lentils are fully cooked. Add the sherry vinegar and whisk in the diced butter. Keep warm until needed. If you need to plan ahead, the lentils can be cooked a day or two in advance and kept in the fridge. If you're doing this don't add the butter until just before serving.

Pre-heat a deep-fat fryer or a large pan of oil to 190°C/375°F or until a cube of bread browns in about 40 seconds.

Sift together the dry ingredients for the spiced flour. In a small bowl mix the cream with the egg white. Dredge the cod fillets in the spiced flour. 'Massage' the fish in the cream mixture, then back again into the flour. Repeat again if you prefer a slightly thicker crust. Carefully drop the cod into the hot oil and cook for about 4 minutes until each fillet is crisp and golden. Drain on kitchen paper.

To serve, spoon a generous amount of lentils on to warmed serving plates and top with the cod and a sprinkling of parsley to garnish.

Breast of Turkey with Leeks, Mushrooms and Sliced Potatoes

THIS DISH IS A FAR CRY FROM THE TURKEY RECIPES THAT NEED TO BE STARTED OFF IN THE MIDDLE OF THE NIGHT IN ORDER TO BE READY FOR LUNCH. YOUNG TURKEY BREASTS DON'T NEED A LONG COOKING TIME, IN FACT THEY CAN BE TREATED BASICALLY THE SAME AS CHICKEN.

SERVES 2

1 turkey breast, about 500 g (1 lb 2 oz)

150 g (5 oz) unsalted butter, chilled and diced

salt and freshly ground black pepper

3 tablespoons vegetable oil

100 g (4 oz) mushrooms, quartered

100 g (4 oz) leeks, sliced 1 cm (½ in) thick

4-6 baby potatoes, par-boiled then sliced

1 tablespoon finely chopped shallot

3 tablespoons dry white wine

50 ml (2 fl oz) water

¼ teaspoon chopped fresh rosemary

Pre-heat the oven to 200°C/400°F/gas 6.

Divide the diced butter into 5 tablespoon portions.

Trim the turkey breast, removing any excess fat. Season generously with salt and pepper. Heat an ovenproof frying-pan over a moderate heat. When hot, add 1 tablespoon of oil and 1 tablespoon of butter. Allow the butter to foam then add the turkey breast skin side down and cook for about 2-3 minutes until the skin is nicely coloured. Turn over for 1 minute to seal the other side. Turn back on to the skin and place in the oven for 20 minutes or until firm to the touch.

While the turkey is roasting, cook the vegetables. Pan-fry the mushrooms over a high heat in 2 tablespoons of butter with a little salt and pepper. In another pan fry the sliced potatoes with 2 tablespoons of oil and 1 tablespoon of butter until golden brown. Cook the leeks in another pan with 1 tablespoon of butter, a good splash of water and a little salt and pepper for about 3 minutes or until the water has evaporated and the leeks are tender. Keep all the vegetables warm.

Remove the turkey from the oven and allow to rest for 5 minutes in a warm place.

To make the sauce, tip any oil from the turkey pan. Add the shallot to the pan over a gentle heat and cook for 2 minutes. Stir in the wine, scraping the bottom of the pan to loosen all the caramelized juices. Boil until almost all the wine has evaporated, then add the water and bring to the boil again. Add the rosemary, then whisk in the remaining butter.

To serve, spoon the vegetables attractively around the outside of warmed plates. Slice the turkey breast and fan the slices in the centre. Top with a little sauce and serve.

OVERLEAF

Dinner for Two for £10, Menu 1: Crispy Fried Cod with Lentils and Vinegar (page 119); Breast of Turkey with Leeks, Mushrooms and Sliced Potatoes (page 120); Stuffed Baked Pear (page 124).

STUFFED BAKED PEAR

THE SWEET PLEASANT TASTE OF A GOOD EATING PEAR NEEDS LITTLE ADORNMENT. THIS SIMPLE FILLING OF ALMOND AND GINGER OFFERS A COMPLEMENTARY ALLIANCE OF FLAVOURS. WE SERVE IT WITH YOGHURT, BUT AN ICE-CREAM WOULD SUIT IT JUST AS WELL. A TIP TO REMEMBER: IF THE PEAR IS VERY ROUNDED AND WILL NOT LAY EASILY IN A HORIZONTAL POSITION, SLICE A LITTLE BIT OFF THE ROUND BEFORE STUFFING IT TO GIVE A LITTLE FLAT BASE ON WHICH TO STAND. THE PASTE STORES WELL IN THE FRIDGE SO WE HAVE GIVEN A QUANTITY THAT WILL SERVE UP TO SIX.

SERVES 2
1 ripe pear, William, Comice
   or Conference
2 teaspoons clear honey
50 g (2 oz) Greek-style
   yoghurt
sprigs of fresh mint to
   garnish (optional)

FOR THE FILLING (FOR SIX)
75 g (3 oz) whole almonds
75 g (3 oz) ginger biscuits
50 g (2 oz) unsalted butter,
   at room temperature
25 g (1 oz) caster sugar
1 egg yolk
juice of ½ lemon

Pre-heat the oven to 190°C/375°F/gas 5.

Make the filling first. Toast the almonds until golden, either under the grill, watching them carefully, or in the pre-heated oven. This only takes a few minutes and really brings out the flavour of the almonds. Chop fairly finely.

Crush the ginger biscuits roughly using a rolling pin or the bottom of a small pan. Mix in the almonds, butter, sugar and egg yolk until the ingredients hold together like a rough paste.

Place the lemon juice in a shallow dish. Peel the pear, rolling in the lemon juice to avoid discolouration. Halve the pear lengthways and core. Pack a full rounded dessert-spoon of the filling on to each pear half. This should fill the cavity and cover most of the exposed half. Place the halves in an ovenproof dish and bake in the pre-heated oven for 15-20 minutes, depending on the ripeness and type of pear used. The pear is cooked when the tip of a knife pierces the centre easily.

To serve, stir the honey into the yoghurt. Place a pear half on each plate and scoop a dollop of the sweetened yoghurt beside it. Garnish with mint if desired.

TOMATO SALAD WITH SHALLOTS, BALSAMIC VINEGAR AND THYME

Ⓥ

A GOOD TOMATO SALAD IS SOMETHING TO REMEMBER. THE SECRET IS GETTING ALL THE SIMPLE THINGS RIGHT. THAT MEANS SUPERB RIPE TOMATOES, SOME FRUITY OLIVE OIL, AND THE RIGHT AMOUNT OF SEASONINGS. LET'S GO!

SERVES 2

2 large ripe tasty tomatoes
salt
$\frac{1}{4}$ teaspoon black pepper, cracked
$\frac{1}{2}$ teaspoon fresh thyme leaves
crusty bread to serve

FOR THE DRESSING

2 tablespoons balsamic vinegar
65 ml (2$\frac{1}{2}$ fl oz) extra virgin olive oil
2 shallots, cut into thin rounds
pinch of salt

To make the dressing, combine all the ingredients in a small bowl and allow it to stand for a least 1 hour. This marinating time pickles the shallots making them mild and less pungent.

Blanch the tomatoes in boiling water for 12 seconds then refresh them under cold water. This process loosens the skin and they should now peel very easily. Carefully slice each tomato, keeping the slices together. Transfer each tomato to a plate as you slice it and press it down domino-style, one slice overlapping the next. Sprinkle each tomato with a little salt, black pepper and thyme leaves. Now generously spoon over the dressing and serve with some nice crusty bread.

SKATE WITH CHILLI AND BASIL CREAM

SKATE IS ONE OF THE FINEST FLAVOURED FISH IN THE SEA. IT'S NOT ESPECIALLY POPULAR IN IRELAND BUT THAT MAY BE DUE TO ITS APPEARANCE, WHICH ISN'T EXACTLY PRETTY. COOKED AS IT IS HERE AND SERVED WITH NEW POTATOES, YOU'LL FIND IT MAKES ONE OF THE MOST DELICIOUS DISHES YOU'VE EVER TASTED.

SERVES 2

2 skate wings about 225 g (8 oz) each, skinned
1 tablespoon unsalted butter
2 shallots, finely chopped
25 g (1 oz) mushrooms, sliced
salt
120 ml (4 fl oz) dry white wine
120 ml (4 fl oz) whipping cream
1 fresh red chilli, seeded and sliced
1 tablespoon chopped fresh basil

Pre-heat the oven to 160°C/325°F/gas 3.

Trim 1 cm (½ in) off the tips of the skate wings with a pair of scissors. Butter a large baking tray and scatter on the shallots and mushrooms. Lay on the skate wings and season with salt. Pour on the wine and cover lightly with foil. Place in the pre-heated oven and cook for about 20 minutes. The time required will depend on how thick the skate wings are. They are cooked when the flesh comes away easily from the bone. Remove the skate from the oven when cooked. Strain the cooking liquid into a clean pan and keep the fish covered while you make the sauce.

Add the cream and chilli to the cooking liquid and bring to the boil. Simmer until the cream thickens to sauce consistency. Add the chopped basil.

To serve, arrange the skate wings on warmed plates with plenty of sauce.

SPICED ROAST CABBAGE

THERE ARE MANY WAYS TO SPICE UP THE LOCAL IRISH GRUB. THIS ONE WAS DISCOVERED BY ACCIDENT BUT WE FIND IT WORKS VERY WELL. CABBAGE, AND IN FACT MOST OF ITS RELATIVES, DOES NOT KEEP VERY WELL WHEN COOKED SO IT IS NOT A GOOD IDEA TO COOK IT TOO FAR IN ADVANCE.

SERVES 2

¼ *savoy cabbage, roughly chopped*
2 tablespoons unsalted butter
1 teaspoon curry powder
salt

Cook the cabbage in boiling salted water for 3 minutes. Drain into a colander then refresh in cold water. Squeeze the cabbage to remove excess water.

Heat the butter in a large frying-pan over moderate heat until it foams. Add the cabbage, curry powder and a little salt. Fry for 3-4 minutes and serve.

PEACH CRUMBLE WITH
RASPBERRY CREAM

SUCH A SCRUMPTIOUS AROMA FILLS THE WHOLE HOUSE WHEN THIS DESSERT IS BAKING IN THE OVEN! IT'S GUARANTEED TO WOO ALL AGES. ALMOST ANY TYPE OF FRUIT CAN BE USED: PEACHES OR NECTARINES, PLUMS OR APPLES, OR TRY TOSSING IN SOME BLACKBERRIES.

SERVES 4

1 kg (2½ lb) fresh ripe
  peaches
50-75 g (2-3 oz) sugar,
  depending on sweetness of
  peaches
1 tablespoon plain flour
grated zest of ½ lemon
65 g (2½ oz) ground
  almonds
65 g (2½ oz) flaked almonds

FOR THE CRUMBLE TOPPING

50 g (2 oz) white caster
  sugar
50 g (2 oz) light brown
  sugar
100 g (4 oz) plain flour
100 g (4 oz) unsalted butter,
  chilled and diced

FOR THE RASPBERRY CREAM

200 g (7 oz) raspberries,
  fresh or frozen
50 g (2 oz) caster sugar
1 teaspoon lemon juice
150 ml (5 fl oz) whipping
  cream

Pre-heat the oven to 190°C/375°F/gas 5.

Halve and peel the peaches. Slice each half into 8 wedges. Toss the peaches with the sugar, flour and lemon zest. Set aside.

To make the topping, work together the sugars, flour and butter with your fingertips until they are sticking together in rough bits about pea-size consistency.

Sprinkle the ground almonds over the bottom of a shallow ovenproof dish. Lay the peaches in next; a depth of about 2.5 cm (1 in) is most suitable. Generously sprinkle on the crumble topping about 1 cm (½ in) thick. Scatter the flaked almonds over the top. Place in the pre-heated oven for about 30 minutes until the top is golden and a knife will pierce the peach flesh easily. Remove from the oven.

To make the raspberry cream, purée the raspberries and sugar in a blender or food processor. Pass the purée though a fine sieve to remove the seeds. Add the lemon juice to the purée. Whip the cream to soft peaks and fold in the purée. Adjust sweetness if necessary by adding a tablespoon or two more of sugar.

To serve, scoop a big spoonful of the peach crumble into a soup plate or shallow bowl and top with a generous spoonful of the raspberry cream. Serve at once, warm rather than hot.

CHAPTER 12

CUPID'S CUISINE

MANY FOODS THROUGHOUT THE YEARS HAVE BEEN CONSIDERED A CATALYST TO LOVE. HOWEVER, FOOD DOESN'T HAVE TO BE AN APHRODISIAC TO REFLECT YOUR FEELINGS. THE TIME TAKEN TO PREPARE SOMETHING SPECIAL SHOWS JUST HOW MUCH YOU CARE. REMEMBER TO KEEP THINGS RATHER LIGHT, FOR A BIG HEAVY MEAL IS ALMOST GUARANTEED TO SEND YOUR LOVER TO SLEEP!

MENU 1

Buttery Stew of Oysters, Asparagus and Leeks
....

Breast of Chicken Stuffed with Lobster and Basil
....

Chocolate and Coconut Torte
....

MENU 2

Cheese Fondue with Asparagus and Broccoli
....

Salmon Baked with Fresh Herbs and Pommes d'Amour
....

White Chocolate Mousse with Mandarin Purée
....

Chocolate Meringues
....

BUTTERY STEW OF OYSTERS, ASPARAGUS AND LEEKS

THIS IS WHAT WE WOULD CALL A SPONTANEOUS DISH FOR THOSE IN THE MOOD, BECAUSE YOU DO NEED TO BE IN THE MOOD FOR OYSTERS!

SERVES 2

10 oysters, shucked and
   reserved in their juices
8 asparagus spears, trimmed
   and lightly peeled
2 tablespoons unsalted butter
2 small leeks, thinly sliced
50 ml (2 fl oz) water
salt and freshly ground white
   pepper
50 ml (2 fl oz) Champagne
   or dry white wine
120 ml (4 fl oz) double
   cream
1 teaspoon lemon juice
1 teaspoon snipped fresh
   chives
1 teaspoon chopped fresh
   chervil
1 teaspoon chopped fresh
   parsley

Check the oysters for pieces of shell. Slice the asparagus on the angle into 2 cm ($^3/_4$ in) lengths.

Place a medium pan over high heat. Add the butter, leeks, asparagus and water to the pan with a little salt. Cook at a rapid boil for 4 minutes. Add the Champagne or wine and cook for a further 2 minutes. Add the cream and bring to the boil. Season with salt and pepper. Add the remaining ingredients. Allow the oysters to warm for about 30 seconds, then serve in warmed bowls.

BREAST OF CHICKEN STUFFED WITH LOBSTER AND BASIL

LOBSTER SEEMS ROMANTIC BECAUSE IT'S SO EXPENSIVE AND EXOTIC. IT IS VERY SEDUCTIVE TO BE WOOED BY THE BEST AND THE MOST EXPENSIVE, SO WE'VE ADDED A BIT OF CHICKEN TO MAKE SURE THAT NO ONE GETS CARRIED AWAY. WE LIKE TO SERVE THIS WITH BUTTERED PASTA. USE FRESH, LIVE LOBSTER IF YOU CAN; IF YOU USE COOKED LOBSTER, MAKE SURE YOU BUY IT VERY FRESH FROM A RELIABLE SOURCE AND OMIT THE FIRST COOKING STAGE.

SERVES 2

1 lobster, about 450 g (1 lb)
2 large chicken fillets, skinless, about 200 g (7 oz) each
100 ml (3½ fl oz) single cream, chilled
1 tablespoon chopped fresh basil
1 tablespoon snipped fresh chives
salt and freshly ground black pepper
1 tablespoon oil

FOR THE SAUCE

shell from the lobster
1 tablespoon olive oil
2 shallots, thinly sliced
2 garlic cloves, crushed
1 tablespoon tomato purée
2 tablespoons port
2 tablespoons brandy
4 tablespoons water
300 ml (10 fl oz) double cream
1 tablespoon chopped fresh basil

Pre-heat the oven to 200°C/400°F/gas 6.

To cook the lobster, bring a large pan of water to a vigorous boil. Put in the lobster, cover and let it cook for about 12 minutes. Remove the lobster from the pan and stop the cooking process by plunging the lobster into a sink of cold water.

Insert a large knife into the lobster at the point where the tail and body are joined and cut towards the tail. The tail meat will now easily pull away from the shell. Break off the arms and claws and crack the shells with a heavy knife. Remove the meat, being careful to discard any pieces of shell. Cut the lobster meat into a 1 cm (½ in) dice.

Remove the inside fillets from the chicken breasts. Remove any sinew from these small fillets with a sharp knife and roughly mash the flesh with a heavy knife or in a blender or food processor. Place this mashed chicken in a bowl and add the lobster, cream, basil, chives, salt and pepper. Beat this mixture vigorously with a wooden spoon until it comes together and looks a little sticky.

To prepare the chicken fillets for stuffing, lay each one flat on a cutting board and make a long horizontal incision almost through the breast so that you can open it out like a book. Season each fillet with a little salt and pepper and spoon the lobster stuffing along the middle line. Fold the two sides on top of the stuffing remoulding it into a good shape with your hands. Butter two sheets of kitchen foil about 25 cm (10 in) square and wrap each breast tightly, twisting the ends to help keep their shape.

Heat a frying-pan over high heat, add the oil, and seal the foil-wrapped fillets for about 4 minutes, turning them every now and then. Place them in the pre-heated oven for about 15 minutes, then remove them and allow to rest in a warm place.

While the chicken is in the oven, make the sauce. First crush the lobster shells with a heavy cleaver or the household hammer. Fry the shells in a pan with the olive oil over high heat for 2 minutes. Add the shallots and garlic and fry for a further 2 minutes. Add the tomato purée, port, brandy and water and allow this to cook until reduced by half. Add the cream and boil until the sauce thickens. Strain the sauce through a fine sieve into a clean pan and add the chopped basil.

To serve, carefully unwrap the chicken breasts, allowing any juices to fall into the sauce. Slice each breast and arrange attractively on warmed plates. Spoon the sauce generously around.

CHOCOLATE AND COCONUT TORTE

THERE IS SOMETHING DEFINITELY ROMANTIC ABOUT CHOCOLATE, AND THIS TASTY LITTLE TORTE WILL HAVE YOUR PARTNER SWOONING IN HIS OR HER SEAT. THIS IS A DESSERT DESIGNED TO IMPRESS. IF YOU ARE NOT A COCONUT-LOVER, SIMPLY SERVE WITH A TRADITIONAL VANILLA CUSTARD. FOR A MORE ELABORATE PRESENTATION, DRIZZLE A CHOCOLATE SAUCE OVER THE TORTE.

SERVES 2

FOR THE TORTE

120 g (4½ oz) plain
  chocolate, finely chopped
90 g (3½ oz) unsalted butter
3 eggs, separated
100 g (4 oz) caster sugar
25 g (1 oz) plain flour

Pre-heat the oven to 190°C/375°F/gas 5. Grease and base line two large ramekins or four 9 cm (3½ in) moulds about 7.5 cm (3 in) deep.

To start the custard, place the milk and coconut in a pan and bring to the boil. Take off the heat and leave to infuse for at least 30 minutes.

Melt the chocolate over a small pan of simmering water. Stir in the butter and set aside. Cream the egg

3-4 *coconut drop macaroons,*
  roughly crushed

250 ml (8 fl oz) *whole milk*
25 g (1 oz) *desiccated*
  coconut
3 *large egg yolks*
60 g (2½ oz) *caster sugar*
¼ *vanilla pod, split, or* ¼
  teaspoon vanilla essence
1 *tablespoon coconut liqueur*

25 g (1 oz) *flaked coconut,*
  toasted
chocolate curls

yolks with 75 g (3 oz) of sugar until light and fluffy then set aside. Whisk the egg whites until they form soft peaks, then add the remaining sugar and whisk vigorously for a further minute or so until the whites are glossy.

Fold the flour gently into the egg yolk mixture, then fold in the melted chocolate, followed by the glossy egg whites. Lastly fold in the crushed macaroons. Fill each mould two-thirds full and bake in the centre of the pre-heated oven for about 15-20 minutes. The little tortes are done when a skewer inserted into the centre comes out moist but not runny. Remove from the oven and leave to cool in the moulds.

To finish the custard, whisk the egg yolks and sugar together in a bowl until light in colour and the sugar has dissolved. Strain the coconut milk. Whisking continuously, slowly pour the strained milk into the egg and sugar mixture.

Pour this mixture back into the pan over a low heat and cook for a few minutes, stirring continously with a wooden spoon until the mixture has thickened enough to coat the back of the spoon and will hold if you run your finger along the middle of the back of the spoon. Strain through a fine sieve then leave to cool.

To serve, unmould the chocolate coconut tortes and place them in the centre of individual plates. Surround with the coconut custard and garnish with toasted coconut flakes and chocolate curls.

OVERLEAF

Cupid's Cuisine, Menu 2: Cheese Fondue with Asparagus and
  Broccoli (page 136); Salmon Baked with Fresh Herbs and
  Pommes d'Amour (page 137); White Chocolate Mousse with
  Mandarin Purée (page 138); Chocolate Meringues (page 139).

CHEESE FONDUE WITH ASPARAGUS AND BROCCOLI

Our friend Bill Hogan in Cork must be one of Ireland's greatest cheese-makers. He is passionate about Swiss cheese-making and, of course, the Swiss-style cheese fondue. He shared with us his simple recipe using his very own Gruyère-style cheese named after the local mountain 'Gabriel' with the soft, rather smelly Irish Durrus cheese.

SERVES 2

200 g (7 oz) Gruyère-style
  cheese such as Gabriel,
  Comte, Emmental
100 g (4 oz) Irish Durrus or
  Raclette
½ garlic clove
150 ml (5 fl oz) dry white
  wine
freshly ground black pepper
200 g (7 oz) asparagus
  spears, cooked
200 g (7 oz) broccoli florets,
  cooked

Cut the cheese into dice 1 cm (½ in) dice. Rub the inside of a fondue dish with the cut side of the garlic. Add the wine and place the dish over a gentle heat. When the wine is warm, add the cheese and stir continuously for about 10 minutes until the cheese has melted. Season with pepper. Help yourself to asparagus or broccoli, dipping it into the melted cheese with your fingers.

If the fondue becomes too thick, thin it by adding a few more spoonfuls of wine.

SALMON BAKED WITH FRESH HERBS AND POMMES D'AMOUR

THIS IS A LIGHT AND ATTRACTIVE DISH WHICH ALLOWS US TO FINISH WITH A SINFULLY RICH DESSERT. IF YOU WANT TO PREPARE THE DISH IN ADVANCE, WILT THE TOMATOES, THE POMMES D'AMOUR, IN THE OVEN, THEN ALLOW THEM TO COOL IN THE BAKING DISH. ADD THE SALMON, COVER WITH FOIL AND CHILL UNTIL REQUIRED. YOU WILL NEED TO ALLOW AN ADDITIONAL 5 MINUTES OVEN TIME TO MAKE SURE THAT THE DISH WARMS THROUGH.

SERVES 2

4 ripe red tomatoes, skinned
½ garlic clove, chopped
75 g (3 oz) unsalted butter
salt and freshly ground white
  pepper
2 fresh salmon fillets,
  skinned and boned, about
  175 g (6 oz) each
1 tablespoon lemon juice
1 teaspoon fresh tarragon
  leaves
1 teaspoon snipped fresh
  chives
1 teaspoon chopped fresh
  parsley
rice or steamed potatoes to
  serve

Pre-heat the oven to 190°C/375°F/gas 5.

Cut the tomatoes in half and gently squeeze out any seeds. Place them in a baking dish about 25 x 20 cm (10 x 8 in) with the garlic, butter and a little salt and pepper. Bake in the pre-heated oven for 10 minutes until the tomatoes are well heated. Season the salmon fillets and add them to the dish, pushing the tomatoes to the outside. Cover with foil and bake for 8-10 minutes or until the salmon is cooked and quite firm. Remove from the oven and mix the lemon juice and the herbs into the buttery tomato juices. Serve on warmed plates with rice or steamed potatoes.

WHITE CHOCOLATE MOUSSE WITH MANDARIN PURÉE

IT IS EXTREMELY DIFFICULT TO MAKE THIS MOUSSE IN A SMALLER QUANTITY AND TO STILL GET THE TEXTURE JUST RIGHT. THEREFORE, WE HAVE GIVEN THE RECIPE IN LARGER QUANTITIES SINCE IT FREEZES REALLY WELL. THE CHOCOLATE MERINGUES (PAGE 139) MAKE A WONDERFUL BASE FOR THE MOUSSE, OFFERING CONTRASTS OF COLOUR AND TEXTURE FOR A MORE COMPLEX AND DRAMATIC DESSERT.

SERVES 6-8

FOR THE MOUSSE

350 g (12 oz) white
   chocolate, chopped
2 leaves gelatine
500 ml (17 fl oz) whipping
   cream
2 eggs
1½ tablespoons Napoleon
   mandarin liqueur

FOR THE MANDARIN PURÉE

1 x 200 g (7 oz) tin
   mandarin segments in
   light syrup
1½ tablespoons Napoleon
   mandarin liqueur
1 tablespoon lemon juice

TO DECORATE

fresh mint sprigs
mandarin segments
   (optional)

To make the mousse, melt the chopped white chocolate over a bowl of simmering but not boiling water, stirring occasionally.

Soften the gelatine in a little cold water for 5 minutes. Whisk the cream until it forms soft peaks; be careful not to whip it too stiffly or the mousse will go dry and granular. Set aside.

Place the eggs in a mixing bowl and whisk over a pan of simmering water for about 5 minutes until light and fluffy. Remove the gelatine from the cold water, squeeze out the excess water and add to the eggs. Continue to whisk over the bain-marie for another minute to ensure that the gelatine has fully dissolved. Remove from the heat and whisk vigorously for 2 minutes or until doubled in volume. Whisking gently, add the melted chocolate in a steady stream until well blended.

Gently whisk in the softly whipped cream, being sure to reach right to the bottom of the bowl as the chocolate has a tendency to sink. Finally, fold in the liqueur.

Place the mousse in the fridge for at least 2 hours to set. This mousse will keep up to three to four days in an airtight container in the fridge.

To prepare the mandarin purée, place all the mandarin pieces and half the tin's syrup in a blender or food processor. Purée then pass through a fine sieve. Adjust thickness of the sauce by adding more syrup if necessary. Stir in the liqueur. Add lemon juice to taste. Set aside.

To serve, use an ice-cream scoop or spoon to put two dollops of mousse on to each plate. Drizzle the purée around. Decorate with mint and a mandarin segment.

CHOCOLATE MERINGUES

THESE FEATHER-LIGHT DISCS OF MERINGUE HAVE AN INTENSE CHOCOLATE FLAVOUR.
THEY CAN BE ENJOYED AS A BISCUIT OR PETIT FOUR IN THEIR OWN RIGHT, OR
SANDWICHED TOGETHER WITH BUTTERCREAM OR GANACHE (A CREAMY CHOCOLATE
MIXTURE), OR EVEN USED TO BUILD MORE COMPLEX DESSERTS. THE SIZE AND SHAPE OF
THEM CAN BE PIPED ACCORDINGLY. THE MERINGUES CAN BE STORED IN AN AIRTIGHT
CONTAINER FOR SEVEN TO TEN DAYS SO IT IS WORTH MAKING THIS QUANTITY.

MAKES ABOUT 12 X 7.5 CM
(3 IN) CIRCLES

3 egg whites
100 g (4 oz) caster sugar
50 g (2 oz) icing sugar,
  sifted
25 g (1 oz) cocoa

Pre-heat the oven to 110°C/225°F/gas ¼. Line a baking sheet with greaseproof paper.

Gently whisk the egg whites for 30 seconds until they begin to froth. Whisk more vigorously until they start to form soft peaks. In a slow, steady stream, add 75 g (3 oz) of the caster sugar. Continue whipping for a further minute until the whites are shiny and thick.

Sift together the rest of the caster sugar, the icing sugar and cocoa. Fold this mixture into the meringue, ensuring that it's all well mixed together.

Using a piping bag with a 1 cm (½ in) nozzle, starred or plain, pipe 7.5 cm (3 in) rounds on to the greaseproof paper. Place in the pre-heated oven and bake slowly for about 2 hours.

These discs should come off the greaseproof easily and be uniformly crisp when they are sufficiently cooked. Remove from the oven and cool.

CHAPTER 13

CUP FINAL DAY

A T THE RISK OF UPSETTING SOME OF OUR LADY FOOT-BALL FANS, A CUP FINAL DAY DOES TEND TO BE, ON THE WHOLE, A BOYS' DAY OUT. THEREFORE WE THINK OF RECIPES OF SUBSTANCE, ITEMS THAT GO WELL WITH BEER - IN LARGE QUANTITIES! IT'S GREAT TO CHOOSE DISHES THAT CAN BE MADE IN ADVANCE AND EASILY RE-HEATED, OR EVEN SERVED AT ROOM TEMPERATURE. SO GIVE THESE RECIPES A GO AND LET THE CELEBRATIONS BEGIN. YOU'LL ENJOY YOUR-SELVES EVEN IF YOU DON'T END UP ON THE WINNING SIDE.

MENU 1

Ham and Cheese Toasties
....

Cheese Quesadillas
....

Spicy Avocado Guacamole
....

Pork Ribs with Spiced Apple Glaze
....

Persian Rice Pilau
....

Chocolate and Banana Ice-cream Pie with Fudge Sauce
....

MENU 2

Blackened Chicken
....

Baked Macaroni with Courgettes, Mushrooms and Cheese
....

Death by Chocolate
....

HAM AND CHEESE TOASTIES

ONE OF THOSE ALL-ROUND FAVOURITES, THIS RECIPE CAN BE VARIED TO SUIT YOUR TASTE; IF YOU PREFER CHEESE AND TOMATO, GO FOR IT! OR TRY AVOCADO AND ALFALFA SPROUTS AND CHEESE, AND SO ON AND SO ON!

MAKES 8

16 slices of bread
100 g (4 oz) unsalted butter,
   at room temperature
400 g Coolea or Gouda-style
   cheese, thinly sliced
400 g (14 oz) ham, sliced
freshly ground black pepper

Pre-heat a cast iron frying-pan over medium heat.

Generously butter one side of each of the slices of bread. Place one slice of bread, butter-side down, into the warm pan. Quickly arrange the cheese and ham slices on to this slice. Season well with the freshly ground pepper and top with another slice - butter-side up! Cook over a medium heat for about 2-3 minutes or until the bottom bread slice is nice and golden. Carefully flip the toasties over and cook on the second side for a further 2 minutes. Lift this toastie out, keep it warm in a low oven and continue to make the rest of the toasties.

To serve, remove the toasties from the oven and cut each one in half. Serve at once.

OVERLEAF

Cup Final Day, Menu 1: Ham and Cheese Toasties (page 141);
Cheese Quesadillas (page 144); Spicy Avocado Guacamole
(page 145); Pork Ribs with Spiced Apple Glaze; (page 146)
Persian Rice Pilau (page 147); Chocolate and Banana
Ice-cream Pie with Fudge Sauce (page 148).

CHEESE QUESADILLAS

CHEESE QUESADILLAS ARE ONE OF THOSE SNACK FOODS THAT ARE EXTREMELY ADDICTIVE. THEY'RE QUICK TO MAKE, NUTRITIOUS AND TASTY. KIDS AND ADULTS LOVE THEM, AND YOU CAN PUT WHATEVER YOU FANCY INTO THEM. YOU CAN BUY READY-MADE TORTILLAS IN GOOD SUPERMARKETS AND DELICATESSENS, AND PICK UP SOME TOMATO SALSA, TOO, TO SERVE WITH WITH CHEESE QUESADILLAS AND THE SPICY AVOCADO GUACAMOLE (PAGE 145).

SERVES 8

16 flour tortillas
4 tablespoons vegetable oil
4 tablespoons unsalted butter
800 g (1¾ lb) Coolea,
    Gouda-style or Cheddar
    cheese, grated

Pre-heat the oven to 150°C/300°F/gas 2.

Pre-heat a heavy-based frying-pan over a medium heat. The butter should sizzle on contact when added. Add ½ tablespoon of butter and ½ tablespoon of oil to the pan. As it melts, lay a tortilla in the pan and quickly sprinkle a handful of the grated cheese into the centre of the tortilla. If it's falling over the edges it will just stick to the pan as it cooks. Lay another tortilla on top and cook over a medium heat for about 2 minutes. The bottom tortilla should be golden brown. Flip over and cook for another minute or so. By the time the second tortilla is golden brown, the cheese should be well melted.

Transfer the tortilla from the frying-pan to some kitchen paper to remove any excess grease. Place in an ovenproof dish in the pre-heated oven and proceed to cook the other quesadillas in the same way.

SPICY AVOCADO GUACAMOLE

Ⓥ

THIS DIP HAS MANY OPTIONS. LEAVE OUT THE CHILLI OR THE TOMATOES, ADD FINELY MINCED ONION OR GREEN PEPPER. WHICHEVER WAY YOU PREFER IT YOU'LL FIND IT HANDY AS A DIP FOR VEGETABLE CRUDITÉS OR QUESADILLAS, AND AS A SPREAD FOR SANDWICHES. IT TASTES BEST WITH ROMA TOMATOES.

SERVES 8
AS A DIP/CONDIMENT

3 ripe avocado

juice of 2 limes

1 garlic clove, finely chopped

5 plum tomatoes, skinned, seeded and chopped

2 tablespoons chopped fresh coriander

1-2 fresh red or green chillies, seeded and finely chopped

salt and freshly ground white pepper

In a small stainless steel or glass bowl, mash the avocado flesh until it is a rough, slightly lumpy purée. A potato masher does a great job, but a wooden spoon will suffice as well. Stir in the lime juice immediately as this preserves the colour. Stir in the garlic, tomatoes and coriander.

Then add the chillies, but remember when adding fresh chilli it is very hard to give exact amounts because the variety of chilli will make a big difference. A general rule of thumb is that green tend to be hotter than red, and smaller are hotter than larger chillies. The best way to approach it is add half a chilli first, taste and adjust as you prefer. Give the avocado a few minutes to absorb the chilli flavour after each addition. Add the salt and pepper to taste.

Use immediately or cover with cling film and place in fridge for up to two to three days.

PORK RIBS WITH SPICED APPLE GLAZE

THIS IS ONE OF THOSE RECIPES WHERE YOU THROW EVERYTHING IN A ROASTING TRAY, BUNG IT IN THE OVEN, SHAKE IT EVERY NOW AND THEN, AND 1½ HOURS LATER YOU HAVE SOMETHING WONDERFUL. IT WILL EMERGE BEAUTIFULLY TENDER WITH A SHINY GLAZE AND EXOTIC FRUIT AROMAS.

SERVES 8

2.25 kg (5 lb) pork ribs

2 tablespoons salt

2 garlic cloves, finely chopped

3 tablespoons grated fresh ginger

3 tablespoons soy sauce

600 ml (1 pint) apple juice

1 large Bramley apple, peeled, cored and sliced

1 tablespoon chilli flakes

4 tablespoons demerara sugar

About 2 hours before cooking (or the night before) season the ribs with the salt, place them in two large roasting tins and leave to stand.

Pre-heat the oven to 200°C/400°F/gas 6.

Mix the remaining ingredients in a large bowl and pour over the ribs. Cover each tray with foil and place in the pre-heated oven for 1 hour. Remove the foil, give each tray a shake and baste the ribs with the juices. Return to the oven without the foil and allow the liquids to reduce to a shining glaze. Continue basting the ribs every 5-10 minutes or so until all the liquid is reduced. Remove from the oven and allow to cool slightly. Chop each side into several portions and serve with finger bowls and plenty of napkins.

PERSIAN RICE PILAU

THE FLAVOURS OF THIS RICE PILAU ADD REAL PIZZAZZ - ESPECIALLY TO THOSE WHO FIND PLAIN RICE BLAND. IT CAN ALSO BE COOKED GENTLY ON TOP OF THE COOKER RATHER THAN IN THE OVEN, IF YOU PREFER. THE AMOUNT OF SALT WILL REALLY DEPEND ON THE VEGETABLE STOCK USED. SOME ARE SO SALTY THAT YOU WILL NOT HAVE TO ADD ANY MORE. TASTE THE RICE WHEN YOU REMOVE IT FROM THE OVEN, AND ADD A LITTLE MORE SALT IF NECESSARY WITH THE SULTANAS AND LEMON ZEST.

SERVES 8

200 g (7 oz) onions, finely chopped
225 g (8 oz) unsalted butter
1 cinnamon stick
1 bay leaf
1 tablespoon finely chopped fresh ginger
1 tablespoon curry powder
550g (1¼ lb) long-grain rice
1.75 litres (3 pints) vegetable stock, hot
100 g (4 oz) sultanas
grated zest of 1 lemon
salt
100 g (4 oz) pine nuts, lightly toasted

Pre-heat the oven to 180°C/350°F/gas 4.

In a large heavy-based ovenproof pan, sweat the onions in the butter over a medium heat for about 5 minutes until they are soft and transparent. Add the cinnamon, bay leaf, ginger and curry powder and sweat gently for another minute.

Add the rice and hot vegetable stock. Bring to the boil over a medium to high heat. Cover with a tight-fitting lid and place in the pre-heated oven for about 10-15 minutes until the rice is tender. Remove from the oven and stir in the sultanas and lemon zest and salt if necessary. Replace the cover and leave the rice to steam in its own heat for 5 minutes. Just before serving, garnish with the toasted pine nuts.

CHOCOLATE AND BANANA ICE-CREAM PIE WITH FUDGE SAUCE

ALTHOUGH THIS ICE-CREAM PIE TAKES A BIT OF TIME AND ORGANIZATION TO MAKE, IT'S A GREAT DESSERT FOR A LARGE GATHERING OF PEOPLE. IT CAN BE MADE A DAY OR TWO AHEAD AND THEN SERVED UP WITH NO FUSS ON THE DAY. THIS WICKED FUDGE SAUCE IS GREAT TO HAVE IN THE FRIDGE TO SERVE WITH SIMPLE BOWLS OF ICE-CREAM, TOO! IN THE STATES, THIS STYLE OF ICE-CREAM PIE IS FREQUENTLY KNOW AS A MUD PIE. MORE THAN SIX HOURS IN THE FREEZER WILL SET THE ICE-CREAM PIE SOLID, SO IT MUST BE ALLOWED TO 'SOFTEN' BEFORE SERVING. THE SAFEST WAY TO DO THIS IS TO PLACE IT IN THE FRIDGE 2-3 HOURS BEFORE SERVING. THE PIE KEEPS WELL IN THE FREEZER IF WRAPPED TIGHTLY IN CLING FILM, SO MAKE THE FULL AMOUNT AND YOU'LL HAVE SOME FOR ANOTHER OCCASION.

SERVES 10-12

FOR THE BASE

150 g (5 oz) pecans
150 g (5 oz) digestive biscuits
100 g (4 oz) unsalted butter, melted
25 g (1 oz) caster sugar

FOR THE FILLING

250 ml (8 fl oz) water
250 g (9 oz) caster sugar
8 egg yolks
200 g (7 oz) milk or plain chocolate
4 bananas, very ripe
1 tablespoon butter
2 tablespoons rum or whiskey (optional)
1 litre (1¾ pints) double cream

Pre-heat the oven to 190°C/375°F/gas 5. Grease and base line a 25 cm (10 in) spring-form cake tin.

If you wish to enhance the flavour of the pecans, toast them in the pre-heated oven for 10-15 minutes.

To make the base, place all the ingredients in a blender or food processor and process until well mixed. Pat this base into the bottom of the prepared tin so that it is about 5 mm (¼ in) thick on the bottom. Pat it about 2 cm (¾ in) up the sides of the tin. Set aside.

To make the filling, place the water and sugar in a small pan and bring to the boil; the sugar will dissolve. Let this syrup cool slightly.

Place the egg yolks in a large bowl that will sit well above a big pan a quarter full of simmering but not boiling water. Don't put the bowl over the water yet, just have it all ready. Melt the chocolate either in a microwave or over a small pan of hot but not boiling water. Set aside.

Peel and roughly chop the bananas. Heat a small frying-pan over a medium heat, add the butter and bananas. Cook until the bananas are very soft and mushy. Take off the heat, add the rum or whiskey, if using, and with a potato masher or a fork, mash the cooked banana to a smooth purée. Set aside.

Whip the double cream to soft peaks.

Whisking continuously, slowly pour the hot syrup on

120 g (4¹/2 oz) plain
  chocolate, finely chopped
40 g (1¹/2 oz) caster sugar
50 ml (2 fl oz) corn or
  golden syrup
50 ml (2 fl oz) water
25 g (1 oz) good quality
  cocoa
2 tablespoons rum or
  whiskey (optional)

to the egg yolks and place the mixture over the prepared pan of simmering water. Continue to whisk for about 10 minutes until the mixture is pale yellow, has quadrupled in volume and trails off the whisk in ribbons. Starting with the syrup fairly hot will take much less time than if the syrup has cooled to room temperature.

Remove from the heat and continue gently whisking this fluffy mixture for several minutes over a large bowl of iced water until cool. Fold in the whipped cream and split the whole mixture equally between two bowls. Fold the melted chocolate into one bowl and the banana purée into the other.

Pour the chocolate filling into the cake tin first; it should fill it about half full. Gently pour the banana mixture over the top until the cake tin is full. Place in the freezer for about 3 hours until set.

To make the fudge sauce, melt the chopped chocolate either in the microwave or in a bowl over a pan of just simmering water. Meanwhile boil the other ingredients for 1-2 minutes, stirring constantly. Remove from heat and leave to cool slightly. Stir in the melted chocolate and rum or whiskey if using. This sauce keeps well in the fridge. Simply heat up in the microwave or heat gently over a small pan of hot water.

To serve, run a hot knife around the cake tin and remove the ring. Using a hot knife, cut slices of the ice-cream pie and place on individual plates. Serve with the warm fudge sauce.

BLACKENED CHICKEN

CHICKEN CAN BE A LITTLE DULL SOMETIMES, BUT NOT SO WITH THIS EXPLOSIVE RECIPE. THE LOUISIANA-STYLE SPICES GIVE US A VERITABLE TORRENT OF FLAVOURS. FABULOUS HOT OR COLD, THIS ONE IS A WINNER!

SERVES 8

8 large chicken fillets,
*   skinless, about 200 g*
*   (7 oz) each*
4 tablespoons vegetable oil·
salad leaves or watercress
*   sprigs to garnish*

BLACKENING SPICES

2 teaspoons salt
2 teaspoons dried oregano
2 teaspoons dried thyme
1 teaspoon black pepper
1 teaspoon white pepper
1 teaspoon onion powder
1 teaspoon garlic powder
1 teaspoon paprika
1 teaspoon cayenne pepper

Pre-heat the oven to 200°C/400°F/gas 6.

In a large bowl, mix together all the blackening spices. Toss the chicken in the spices, making sure that each fillet is evenly coated. Heat a large heavy frying-pan over a high heat until very hot. Add the oil and fry the chicken fillets on each side. You want the chicken to fry quite fast so that you sear and roast the spices very well. Don't be tempted to add too many fillets to the pan at once or you will not get the desired effect. When each fillet is well seared, place on a roasting tray and bake in the pre-heated oven for 10 minutes.

Serve the chicken on a platter garnished with a few salad leaves or watercress.

BAKED MACARONI WITH COURGETTES, MUSHROOMS AND CHEESE

MACARONI SHOULD NEVER GO OUT OF FASHION. COOKING A DISH LIKE THIS REMINDS YOU HOW SATISFYING AND VERSATILE THIS LITTLE PASTA SHAPE IS. OF COURSE, YOU MAY USE PENNE, RIGATONI, FUSILLI OR WHATEVER OTHER SHAPE YOU CHOOSE, BUT SOMEHOW THEY ARE NOT QUITE AS COMFORTING.

SERVES 8

4 tablespoons olive oil

4 tablespoons unsalted butter

8 medium courgettes, cut into 2 cm ($^3/_4$ in) dice

salt and freshly ground black pepper

750 g (1$^1/_2$ lb) button mushrooms, quartered

550 g (1$^1/_4$ lb) macaroni

150 g (5 oz) unsalted butter

500 ml (17 fl oz) whipping cream

200 g (7 oz) mild Cheddar, grated

200 g (7 oz) Parmesan, freshly grated

Pre-heat the oven to 190°C/375°F/gas 5. Lightly butter a large baking dish about 36 x 20 cm (14 x 8 in).

Heat half the oil and butter in a large frying-pan over a high heat until the butter is foaming. Add the courgettes, season with a little salt and pepper and fry until lightly browned and just cooked. Tip the courgettes into a colander then fry the mushrooms in the same way.

Bring 5 litres (9 pints) of salted water to the boil in a large pan. Add the macaroni, stir well and cook until just *al dente*. Drain well.

While the macaroni is draining, add the butter and cream to the pan and bring to the boil. Return the macaroni to the pan with the mushrooms, courgettes and half the cheeses. Check and adjust the seasoning to taste. Tip everything into the baking dish. Sprinkle with the remaining cheese and bake in the pre-heated oven for about 15 minutes.

DEATH BY CHOCOLATE

THIS IS ONE DESSERT THAT WILL SATISFY EVEN THE MOST DIE-HARD CHOCOHOLIC: SMOOTH, INTENSE AND INDESCRIBABLY DELICIOUS! TRY IT AND SEE. IF YOU WISH, THE TERRINE CAN BE DECORATED WITH WHIPPED CREAM, RASPBERRY SAUCE (PAGE 80) OR EVEN CHOCOLATE SAUCE (PAGE 183).

SERVES 8-10

450 g (1 lb) plain chocolate, chopped

250 ml (8 fl oz) whipping cream

50 g (2 oz) unsalted butter

4 egg yolks

120 g (5 oz) icing sugar, sifted

120 ml (4 fl oz) Irish whiskey or liqueur

Line a 1 litre (1¾ pint) terrine with cling film, letting it hang generously over all four sides.

Place chocolate, cream and butter in a medium bowl and place over a pan of just simmering water. Stir occasionally until the chocolate and butter have melted and mixed together. Remove from the heat and slowly whisk in the egg yolks. Slowly stir in the icing sugar and continue to stir gently until the mixture is smooth, shiny and homogenous. Stir in the whiskey or your chosen liqueur.

Pour into the prepared terrine and smooth out to fill the mould. Tap the mould on the worktop once or twice to remove any air bubbles. Cover with the cling film and chill overnight.

To serve, unmould by turning upside down on to a chopping board or other flat surface. Cut into slices with a hot knife.

CHAPTER 14

LEAN TIMES

OUR SOCIETY IS IN THE GRIP OF A FITNESS AND HEALTH REVIVAL. THIS CAN BE INTIMIDATING AT FIRST BECAUSE THERE IS A LOT TO THINK ABOUT: HOW DO I COOK LOW FAT FOOD, HOW CAN I BECOME NUTRITIONALLY AWARE? TAKE IT ONE STEP AT A TIME. IT'S SURPRISING HOW EASY IT CAN BE WHEN YOU UNDERSTAND THE BASIC BREAKDOWN OF FOODSTUFFS. YOU'LL NOTICE RIGHT AWAY THAT HERBS, SPICES AND FLAVOURINGS BECOME A VERY IMPORTANT AND EXCITING PART OF DISHES.

MENU 1

Carrageen Tomato Mousse
....

Salad of Green Beans
....

Ostrich Satay
....

Savoury Vegetable Pancakes
....

Ruby Grapefruit and Juniper Granita
....

MENU 2

Mussels with Potato and Garlic
....

*Grilled Chicken with Lemon, Black Pepper
and Red Onion*
....

Warm Lentil and Fennel Salad
....

Fresh Papaya with Coconut Yoghurt Cream
....

CARRAGEEN TOMATO MOUSSE

CARRAGEEN IS AN IRISH SEAWEED THAT IS WELL KNOWN FOR ITS GELATINOUS AND NUTRITIOUS QUALITIES. IF PROPERLY PREPARED IT DOESN'T TASTE AT ALL OF THE SEA AND CAN EVEN BE USED IN DESSERTS. IT IS READILY AVAILABLE IN HEALTH FOOD SHOPS.

SERVES 4-6

25 g (1 oz) carrageen moss
    or 4 teaspoons powdered
    gelatine
1 tablespoon light olive oil
2 tablespoons shallots, sliced
1 tablespoon chopped garlic
550 g (1¼ lb) very ripe
    tomatoes, quartered
50 g (2 oz) double tomato
    concentrate
½ large red pepper, seeded
    and sliced
1 tablespoon tomato ketchup
20 drops tabasco sauce
1 tablespoon chopped fresh
    tarragon
5 egg whites
salt and freshly ground black
    pepper

Wash the carrageen moss and soak it in cold water for about 30 minutes or until it swells to double its size. Drain it in a colander and squeeze dry. It is now ready to use. Alternatively, dissolve the gelatine in a little cold water.

In a large pan, heat the oil and sweat the shallots and garlic for about 3 minutes until soft. Add the remaining ingredients except the carrageen moss, tarragon and egg whites. Add a little salt and mash the tomatoes with a spoon to encourage them to release their juice. Bring to the boil and simmer for about 5 minutes. Add the carrageen moss or gelatine, cover and cook gently for 15 minutes. Tip the tomato mixture into a blender or food processor and purée until smooth. Pass through a sieve into a clean bowl, add the tarragon and a little pepper and allow to cool to room temperature.

Whisk the egg whites in a clean bowl until they form soft peaks. Fold about one-third of the egg whites into the tomato mixture with a spatula. Then carefully fold in the remainder, cover and chill for at least 6 hours.

To serve, dip a soup spoon or an ice-cream scoop into hot water then scoop the mousse into the centre of individual plates.

SALAD OF GREEN BEANS

WHEN PROPERLY PREPARED, A SIMPLE SALAD OF GREEN BEANS CAN BE STUNNING. WE FEEL THAT IT IS IMPORTANT TO COOK THE BEANS ENOUGH SO THAT THEY ARE NOT CRUNCHY OR SQUEAKY TO EAT. COOKED UNTIL JUST TENDER, THEY HAVE MUCH MORE FLAVOUR AND CHARACTER. IF YOU ARE PREPARING THIS IN ADVANCE, DON'T COMBINE THE BEANS WITH THE DRESSING UNTIL THE LAST MOMENT OR THEY WILL GO GREY.

SERVES 4

200 g (7 oz) green beans
2 shallots, finely chopped
$\frac{1}{2}$ teaspoon finely chopped
  garlic
4 tablespoons Standard
  Vinaigrette (page 178)
salt and freshly ground black
  pepper

Bring a pan of lightly salted water to the boil. Taste the water. If it doesn't taste lightly salty, add more salt. Add the green beans and cook at a rolling boil for about 8-10 minutes until tender. Drain in a colander, refresh in plenty of cold water, then allow to cool while you make the dressing.

In a small bowl combine the shallots, garlic and vinaigrette. Add the beans to the dressing and toss to coat evenly. Serve immediately with a few twists of pepper.

OSTRICH SATAY

IRISH OSTRICH FARMERS ARE HAILING OSTRICH AS THE PERFECT MEAT. LOWER IN FAT
THAN CHICKEN AND HIGHER IN PROTEIN THAN BEEF, IT VERY WELL MIGHT BE. ALL OF
OUR 'GUINEA PIGS' LOVED IT, PROCLAIMING IT TO BE QUITE LIKE BEEF. NEEDLESS TO SAY
YOU CAN SUBSTITUTE BEEF FILLET FOR THE OSTRICH VERY SUCCESSFULLY.
MANGETOUTS MAKE A GOOD ACCOMPANIMENT.

SERVES 4

600 g (1½ lb) ostrich or beef
fillet
1 tablespoon vegetable oil

FOR THE MARINADE

4 tablespoons dark soy sauce
1½ tablespoons curry
powder
2 tablespoons clear honey
pinch of white pepper
1 tablespoon peanut oil

Slice the fillet in eight medallions. Combine all the
marinade ingredients in a bowl. Add the meat, rubbing
the marinade into the meat with your fingers. Allow the
meat to marinate for a least 4 hours or preferably
overnight in the fridge.

Heat a large non-stick frying-pan over a high heat. Add
a little vegetable oil, then four medallions and cook for
about 2 minutes on each side for medium rare or 4 for
well done. Allow the medallions to rest in a warm place
while you finish cooking the remaining pieces. When all
are cooked, scrape any remaining marinade into the pan
and add a few tablespoons of water. This will give a little
bit of sauce to drizzle over the finished dish.

SAVOURY VEGETABLE PANCAKES

Ⓥ

THESE LEAN, HIGH-FIBRE PANCAKES ARE THE PERFECT ACCOMPANIMENT TO GRILLED MEATS, OR THEY WOULD ALSO WORK WELL WITH ORIENTAL FISH RECIPES LIKE THE GLAZED MONKFISH WITH BLACK PEPPER AND GINGER (PAGE 79).

SERVES 4-6

1 egg white

salt

$\frac{1}{2}$ garlic clove, crushed and
  chopped

200 g (7 oz) courgettes,
  grated

100 g (4 oz) carrots, grated

100 g (4 oz) celeriac, grated

100 g (4 oz) mushrooms,
  finely chopped

1 tablespoon chopped onion

1 teaspoon finely grated
  fresh ginger

$\frac{1}{4}$ teaspoon curry powder

3 tablespoons breadcrumbs

2 tablespoons wholewheat
  flour

freshly ground black pepper

4 tablespoons vegetable oil

Lightly whisk the egg white with a pinch of salt and the garlic. Add the remaining ingredients except the vegetable oil.

Heat a large non-stick frying-pan over a medium heat. Brush a little of the oil over the frying-pan. Drop 2 tablespoon mounds of the pancake mixture into the pan. Pat each mound out to form a pancake about 6 cm ($2\frac{1}{2}$ in) in diameter. Cook the pancakes for about 3 minutes on each side until they are lightly browned. Transfer the pancakes to a baking sheet and keep them warm in a low oven. Cook the remaining mixture in the same way.

RUBY GRAPEFRUIT AND JUNIPER GRANITA

THE CLEAR, UNADULTERATED FLAVOUR OF THIS GRANITA IS IMMENSELY REFRESHING. IN FACT IT'S ONE OF PAUL'S FAVOURITE DESSERTS. PURE AND SIMPLE. USE TALL WIDE-RIMMED GLASSES LIKE MARTINI GLASSES IF POSSIBLE, AND CHILL THEM BEFORE SERVING SO THAT THE GRANITA DOES NOT MELT SO QUICKLY.

SERVES 4-6

320 ml (11 fl oz) water

200 g (7 oz) caster sugar

about 6 juniper berries,
    lightly crushed

2 ruby grapefruit

250 ml (8 fl oz) fresh ruby
    grapefruit juice

1½ tablespoons gin

Place the 120 ml (4 fl oz) of water, 50 g (2 oz) of sugar and the juniper berries in a pan and bring to the boil. Remove from the heat and leave to infuse for 30 minutes.

In another small pan, bring the remaining water and sugar to the boil then remove from the heat and leave to cool.

Segment the grapefruit so as to remove all the skin, pith and seeds. Place the grapefruit segments in the second sugar solution and chill in the fridge.

Strain the sugar water and juniper berries through a fine sieve into the grapefruit juice then add the gin. Pour this into a wide shallow metal container and place in the freezer for about 1 hour until the granita starts to freeze and form crystals. Scrape the sides and mix gently to combine the more frozen parts with the less frozen. A true granita texture is formed by stirring occasionally while freezing; this forms the tiny crystals of ice. It will take about 3 hours for it all to set sufficiently.

To serve, place a few of the grapefruit segments in each glass. Scoop in a spoonful or two of the granita and top with a couple more segments. Serve at once!

MUSSELS WITH POTATO AND GARLIC

MUSSELS ARE SO TASTY THAT THEY REQUIRE VERY LITTLE EMBELLISHMENT. HERE THEY ARE PARTNERED WITH GARLIC POTATOES AND HERBS TO GIVE A GUTSY LOW-FAT TREAT. IT IS IMPORTANT NOT TO BOIL THE MUSSELS TOO MUCH OR THEY WILL GO TOUGH. ADD A SPLASH OF DOUBLE CREAM AT THE LAST MOMENT FOR EXTRA LUXURY.

SERVES 4

1.5 kg (3½ lb) live mussels
200 ml (7 fl oz) water
50 ml (2 fl oz) dry white wine
1 sprig of fresh thyme
1 sprig of fresh parsley
3 garlic cloves, sliced
100 g (4 oz) leeks, thinly sliced
400 g (14 oz) potatoes, peeled and cut into 1 cm (½ in) dice
1 tablespoon chopped fresh parsley
freshly ground black pepper

Wash the mussels in plenty of cold water, pulling away the hairy beards as you go. Discard any that are not closed or do not close when tapped sharply with a knife. Bring the water and white wine to the boil in a large pan. Add the herb sprigs and garlic and simmer for 1 minute. Add the mussels, bring to a vigorous boil and cook for 4-5 minutes or until they have all opened. Discard any mussels that have not opened. Immediately drain into a colander catching all the juices in a bowl underneath.

Strain the juices into a clean pan and add the leeks and potatoes. Cook over a moderate heat for about 7 minutes or until the potatoes are tender.

While the potatoes are cooking, pull the mussels from their shells. Save a few of the shells for garnish.

To serve, add the mussels and chopped parsley to the potato broth and warm thoroughly. Check and adjust the seasoning to taste. Serve in warmed bowls garnished with a few nice shells.

GRILLED CHICKEN WITH LEMON, BLACK PEPPER AND RED ONION

THIS ZESTY LITTLE DISH CAN BE WHIPPED UP IN MINUTES, BUT IT DOES IMPROVE IF YOU HAVE THE TIME TO LET IT MARINATE. YOU CAN FIND PRESERVED LEMONS IN MOST LARGE SUPERMARKETS AND IN ASIAN OR MIDDLE EASTERN GROCERIES.

SERVES 4

4 chicken fillets, boneless, skinned and 200 g (7 oz) each

1 preserved lemon, finely chopped

1 red onion, finely chopped

1 teaspoon black pepper, cracked

½ teaspoon chilli flakes (optional)

1 tablespoon chopped fresh parsley

2 tablespoons olive oil

1 teaspoon clear honey

1 teaspoon salt

a few mixed salad leaves to serve

Pre-heat the grill to its highest setting.

Combine all the ingredients in a large bowl and toss thoroughly. If you have the time, allow it to marinate for a few hours in the fridge.

Place the chicken flat on a grill tray. Make sure that the chicken pieces are well coated with the little pieces of onion and lemon and so on as this gives a beautiful colour. Place under the grill and cook for 7-10 minutes on each side until the chicken is firm and completely cooked. Serve garnished with a few mixed salad leaves.

WARM LENTIL AND FENNEL SALAD

LENTILS ARE DEFINITELY ONE OF THE FOODS OF THE MOMENT. BROWN OR GREEN LENTILS WORK BEST FOR THIS RECIPE AND BOTH ARE READILY AVAILABLE. THIS SALAD CAN EASILY BE MADE A DAY OR TWO AHEAD AND THEN SERVED WARM OR COLD.

SERVES 4

225 g (8 oz) green lentils

600 ml (1 pint) water

1 teaspoon salt

1 sprig of fresh thyme or
  $^1/_2$ teaspoon dried thyme

1 sprig of fresh parsley

1 small onion, finely chopped

1 small carrot, finely
  chopped

1 fennel bulb, finely chopped

3 tablespoons balsamic
  vinegar or $1^1/_2$ tablespoons
  white wine vinegar

5 tablespoons olive oil

1 tablespoon chopped fresh
  parsley

1 teaspoon black pepper,
  cracked

Rinse the lentils in plenty of cold water. Place them in a pan with the water and salt. Bring to the boil and simmer for 5 minutes, skimming off any scum that rises to the surface. Add the herb sprigs and vegetables and simmer for a further 15 minutes, by which time the lentils should be cooked. Drain off any excess water and allow the lentils to cool slightly. Finally stir in the remaining ingredients and serve warm.

OVERLEAF

Lean Times, Menu 2: Mussels with Potato and Garlic (page 159); Grilled Chicken with Lemon, Black Pepper and Red Onion (page 160); Warm Lentil and Fennel Salad (page 161); Fresh Papaya with Coconut Yogurt Cream (page 164).

FRESH PAPAYA WITH COCONUT YOGHURT CREAM

GOOD QUALITY PAPAYAS ARE WIDELY AVAILABLE NOW; JUST BE SURE TO USE RIPE ONES AS THEIR FLAVOUR WILL BE FULLY DEVELOPED. WHAT COULD BE SIMPLER THAN SLICING UP A GORGEOUS PIECE OF FRUIT AND DRESSING IT WITH COMPLEMENTARY FLAVOURS? MANGOES COULD BE SUBSTITUTED FOR A CHANGE.

SERVES 4

2 fresh ripe papaya
juice of 1 lime
200 ml (7 fl oz) coconut milk
250 ml (8 fl oz) thick-set,
    Greek-style yoghurt
4 tablespoons caster sugar
2 tablespoons coconut flakes,
    toasted (optional)

Halve, peel and seed the papayas. Slice each half attractively and arrange on individual serving plates. Sprinkle liberally with lime juice to taste.

Stir about 120 ml (4 fl oz) of coconut milk into the yoghurt. Taste. Each brand of coconut milk seems to be different, so this is a starting amount. Add more as needed. A couple tablespoons of sugar really brings up the flavours (although not absolutely necessary if you're on a strict diet) so stir in 3-4 tablespoons of sugar and taste again. Really just a hint of sweetness is all the cream needs.

Scoop a dollop of the yoghurt cream on to each plate beside the papaya slices and decorate with toasted coconut flakes if desired.

CHAPTER 15

MEATLESS MEALS

MANY CARNIVORES HAVE NEVER EATEN A GOOD VEGETARIAN MEAL, AND BELIEVE THAT IF THEY GAVE UP MEAT THEY WOULD SUFFER NUTRITIONALLY. THIS IS FALSE. A GOOD VEGETARIAN MEAL CAN BE COMPLETELY SATISFYING. THERE ARE NO DIETARY PROBLEMS WITH A SOUND VEGETARIAN DIET: WITH PROPER KNOWLEDGE IT CAN BE AS BALANCED AS ANY. WITH TODAY'S LOW STANDARD OF HEALTH AND THE HIGH COST OF MEAT, PERHAPS IT'S AN ISSUE THAT MORE PEOPLE SHOULD BE THINKING ABOUT.

MENU 1

Roast Pumpkin Soup with Fresh Thyme
....

Gruyère and Parmesan Cheese Toasts
....

Risotto Primavera
....

Salad of Herbs
....

Buttered Apples on Sugar-glazed Barmbrack
....

MENU 2

Mushroom and Aubergine Tart with Garlic Chives
....

Penne with Broccoli, Goats' Cheese and Sun-dried Tomatoes
....

Kiwi Soup with Passion Fruit Ice-cream
....

ROAST PUMPKIN SOUP WITH FRESH THYME

PUMPKIN IS A WONDERFUL WINTER VEGETABLE WHICH LENDS ITSELF TO A GREAT VARIETY OF RECIPES. IT'S WORTH GETTING TO KNOW AND THIS SOUP IS A GOOD STARTING POINT. EXPERIMENT WITH DIFFERENT VARIETIES, AS SOME CAN BE VERY BLAND WHILE OTHERS ARE RICH AND CONCENTRATED. BUTTER NUT AND ACORN ARE TWO OF OUR FAVOURITES. THE SOUP WILL KEEP IN AN AIRTIGHT CONTAINER IN THE FRIDGE FOR SEVERAL DAYS.

SERVES 6

1 kg (2^1/$_4$ lb) pumpkin, halved and seeded

4^1/$_2$ tablespoons unsalted butter

750 g (1^1/$_2$ lb) onions, roughly chopped

3 garlic cloves, finely chopped

750 ml (1^1/$_4$ pints) vegetable stock

1 bouquet garni

pinch of freshly grated nutmeg

pinch of cayenne pepper

salt and freshly ground white pepper

375 ml (13 fl oz) milk

1 tablespoon fresh thyme leaves or ^{1}/$_2$ tablespoon dried thyme

Gruyère and Parmesan Cheese Toasts (page 167) to serve

Pre-heat the oven to 200°C/400°F/gas 6.

Place the pieces of seeded pumpkin flesh-side down on a large baking sheet. Cover tightly with kitchen foil and cook in the pre-heated oven for about 1 hour until the flesh is soft to the touch. Remove from the oven, scoop all the flesh off the pumpkin shell and set aside.

Melt the butter in a large pan over a medium high heat and sweat the onions and garlic for about 5 minutes until soft and transparent without any colouring. Add the cooked pumpkin flesh and vegetable stock, and all the seasonings except the thyme. Bring it all up to the boil, then simmer gently for about 10 minutes. As the pumpkin and onion are already cooked you're really just letting the flavours meld together at this point. Remove from the heat and leave to cool slightly. Purée in a blender or food processor then pass through a fine sieve.

Return to a clean pan, add the milk and thyme, then re-heat the soup over a medium heat without allowing it to boil. Serve immediately in warmed soup bowls with the Gruyère and Parmesan Cheese Toasts on the side, or even placed on top just before serving.

GRUYÈRE AND PARMESAN CHEESE TOASTS

A GRILLED CHEESE TOAST IS SO SIMPLE AND YET SO TASTY. SERVE WITH SOUP, OR EVEN FLOATING ON A SOUP, WITH A SALAD OR SIMPLE VEGETABLE DISH. THE PASTE KEEPS WELL IN THE FRIDGE FOR SEVERAL DAYS AND CAN BE EXTREMELY USEFUL TO HAVE ON HAND.

SERVES 6

100 g (4 oz) Gabriel or Gruyère-style cheese, finely grated

90 g (3½ oz) Parmesan, finely grated

120 g (4½ oz) unsalted butter, softened

6 slices country-style bread, 2 cm (¾ in) thick

Pre-heat the grill to high.

In a bowl, work the two cheeses together with the butter until you have a cohesive paste. Lightly toast the bread slices on each side. Spread a generous amount of the cheese paste on to each slice, at least 5 mm (¼ in) thick. Place the toasts under the grill for 1-2 minutes and watch carefully. They are done when the top is golden brown and bubbly. Serve immediately.

RISOTTO PRIMAVERA

A CREAMY RISOTTO LIKE THIS CAN LEND ITSELF TO ANY MIXTURE OF VEGETABLES SO FEEL FREE TO EXPERIMENT AND USE WHAT YOU PREFER OR HAVE AVAILABLE. WE THINK ALMOST EVERY VEGETARIAN WOULD ENJOY A DISH SUCH AS THIS, BUT IS CAN ALSO BE SERVED AS AN ACCOMPANIMENT TO GRILLED CHICKEN, MEAT OR FISH.

SERVES 6

100 g (4 oz) onions, finely chopped

50 g (2 oz) unsalted butter

450 g (1 lb) arborio or risotto rice

1.2 litres (2 pints) vegetable stock, hot

salt

200 g (7 oz) mushrooms, quartered

200 g (7 oz) courgettes, sliced about 3 cm (1 1/4 in) thick

100 g (4 oz) fresh peas

200 g (7 oz) broccoli florets

5 plum tomatoes, skinned and seeded

50 g (2 oz) Parmesan, finely grated

60 g (2 1/2 oz) butter, chilled and diced

TO GARNISH

fresh herbs such as chervil, parsley, basil or coriander

freshly grated Parmesan

In a heavy-based pan over medium heat gently sweat the onions in 30 g (1 1/2 oz) of butter until soft and transparent. Stir in the rice and stir gently for about 2 minutes. Reduce the heat to medium and add a ladle at a time of the vegetable stock. Stir fairly continuously and wait each time until nearly all the liquid has been absorbed before adding more. After about 15-20 minutes, the rice should be cooked and all the liquid added and absorbed. Check and season to taste with salt (vegetable stock cubes can be very salty, so taste before seasoning). Set aside.

Melt the remaining butter over a medium to high heat and gently fry the mushroom and courgettes. Strain into a colander, season with salt and reserve in a warm place.

Bring a pan of water to the boil, add the peas and broccoli florets, return to the boil and blanch for 1 minute. Drain. Arrange them in an oven tray with the tomatoes and heat through in a hot oven or in a microwave for about 1 minute on medium power.

Stir the Parmesan and 50 g (2 oz) of cold diced butter into the risotto. Add all the warmed vegetables and stir to distribute evenly.

To serve, scoop on to warmed plates and serve immediately. Garnish with fresh herbs if desired and pass around an extra bowl of freshly grated Parmesan.

SALAD OF HERBS

FRESH HERBS LIBERALLY SPRINKLED THROUGH SALAD LEAVES GIVES A WHOLE NEW DIMENSION TO A SALAD.

SERVES 4-6

200 g (7 oz) mixed salad
leaves
50 g (2 oz) chopped fresh
herbs such as snipped
chives, chervil sprigs,
flatleaf parsley sprigs,
tarragon
3-4 tablespoons Standard
Vinaigrette (page 178)

Simply sprinkle the herbs over the salad leaves, then toss the leaves in the vinaigrette and serve immediately.

BUTTERED APPLES ON SUGAR-GLAZED BARMBRACK

BARMBRACK IS THE IRISH EQUIVALENT OF A YEASTED FRUIT LOAF. BRIOCHE WOULD BE A WONDERFUL SUBSTITUTE, BUT A GOOD QUALITY WHITE LOAF WOULD BE FINE TOO. SWEETENING THE CREAM AND FLAVOURING IT WITH A DASH OF VANILLA ESSENCE MAKES A DELICIOUS CHANTILLY CREAM WHICH IS PERFECT WITH THE BARMBRACK.

SERVES 6

1 loaf barmbrack, fruit loaf
or white bread
100 g (4 oz) unsalted butter
60 g (2½ oz) icing sugar,
sifted
600 g (1¼ lb) Bramley
cooking apples
juice of 1 lemon
150 g (5 oz) unsalted butter
100 g (4 oz) caster sugar
450 ml (15 fl oz) whipping
cream
few drops of vanilla essence

Pre-heat the grill to high.

To prepare the barmbrack. Slice the loaf into 1 cm (½ in) thick slices. Either cut the crusts off and have a neat rectangle shape, or use a large pastry cutter and cut big rounds. Spread each side with butter and evenly sprinkle on some of the icing sugar. Set aside.

Peel and core the apples, rolling each in the lemon juice to avoid discoloration. Halve and cut each half into four even wedges.

Heat a large heavy-based frying-pan over a medium heat and add the butter. After it has foamed, toss in half the sugar and stir constantly until it turns a nice medium caramel colour. Toss in the apples and cook over medium to high heat for about 5 minutes, stirring and turning continuously, until the apples are a rich golden hue and can be pierced easily with a fork. If you don't have a large frying-pan, cook in two batches to ensure even cooking and proper colouring of the apples. Remove the pan from the heat.

Place the buttered and sugared slices of barmbrack under the pre-heated grill and watch closely. You just want an even golden toasting. Turn over and glaze the other side in the same manner.

Whip the cream until it holds fairly firm peaks, then fold in the remaining sugar and the vanilla essence.

To serve, place the glazed barmbrack on to warmed plates and spoon a generous portion of the buttered apples on top. Scoop a dollop of the chantilly cream on top and serve immediately.

MUSHROOM AND AUBERGINE TART WITH GARLIC CHIVES

Ⓥ

THE RICH FLAVOURS OF MUSHROOMS, AUBERGINE AND A LITTLE GARLIC HERE ARE SIMPLY DELICIOUS. HOWEVER THIS IS A VERY VERSATILE TART WHICH CAN BE USED AS A BASE RECIPE - SIMPLY CHANGE THE VEGETABLES WITH THE SEASONS. GARLIC CHIVES ARE AVAILABLE IN MOST ASIAN SUPERMARKETS. FOR A DELICIOUS LUNCH FOR FOUR PEOPLE, SERVE THE TART WITH THE SALAD OF HERBS (PAGE 169).

SERVES 6

225 g (8 oz) Savoury Pastry
  (page 177)
40 g (1½ oz) unsalted butter
100 ml (3½ fl oz) olive oil
300 g (12 oz) button
  mushrooms, quartered
salt and freshly ground black
  pepper
400 g (14 oz) aubergines,
  cut into a 1 cm (½ in) dice
2 tablespoons snipped fresh
  garlic chives or 3 garlic
  cloves, chopped
3 eggs
3 egg yolks
450 ml (15 fl oz) single
  cream

Pre-heat the oven to 180°C/350°F/gas 4. Grease a 20 cm (8 in) tart tin.

Roll out the pastry and use it to line the prepared tart tin. Place in the fridge to chill for at least 20 minutes. Cover with kitchen foil, fill with baking beans and bake blind in the pre-heated oven for about 10 minutes until light golden brown. Remove the foil and beans and set the tart aside to cool.

Reduce the oven temperature to 150°C/300°F/gas 2.

In a large frying-pan heat the butter and 1 tablespoon of oil until foaming. Add the mushrooms and fry until cooked. Season with salt and pepper and tip into a large bowl. Heat the remaining olive oil and fry the aubergines with a little salt over a moderately high heat. Don't be tempted to add more olive oil as this will make the whole dish too oily. Fry the aubergines until light brown and cooked through. Add the aubergines to the mushrooms and mix in the garlic chives or garlic.

In a medium bowl, whisk the eggs and egg yolks together until well blended. Add the cream, ½ teaspoon of salt and a pinch of pepper and whisk gently until you have a smooth mixture. Stir in the mushrooms and aubergines. Gently pour the filling into the pastry case and cook in the pre-heated oven for about 40 minutes until the tart is completely set. Allow to cool for 10 minutes before serving.

Penne with Broccoli, Goats' Cheese and Sun-dried Tomatoes

WITH A SATISFYING RECIPE LIKE THIS ONE, WHO NEEDS MEAT? THE TOMATOES AND THE CHEESE MAKE IT RICH AND FILLING, WHILE THE BROCCOLI ADDS TEXTURE AND VARIETY. TRY SUBSTITUTING OTHER VEGETABLES SUCH AS ASPARAGUS OR FENNEL.

SERVES 6

550 g (1¼ lb) penne

750 g (1½ lb) broccoli florets, cooked

300 g (11 oz) sun-dried tomatoes in oil, chopped

250 g (9 oz) goats' cheese, skin removed and crumbled

175 ml (6 fl oz) virgin olive oil

salt and freshly ground black pepper

Bring 5 litres (9 pints) of water to the boil in a large pan. Add the penne and cook until just *al dente*. Just before you drain the penne, add the cooked broccoli florets, wait for 15 seconds then drain into a colander.

Return the pasta and broccoli to the hot pan and add the tomatoes, cheese, olive oil and some freshly ground black pepper. Check and adjust the seasoning to taste and serve immediately on warmed plates.

Kiwi Soup with Passion Fruit Ice-cream

THIS LIGHT, TANGY DESSERT WITH ITS CLEAN, BOLD FLAVOURS AND COLOURS IS REALLY REFRESHING. A LEMON SORBET COULD BE SUBSTITUTED FOR THE ICE-CREAM WHICH WOULD MAKE IT A VERY LOW-FAT DESSERT OPTION. FOR A RICHER ICE-CREAM, REPLACE HALF THE MILK WITH WHIPPING CREAM.

SERVES 6

120 ml (4 fl oz) passion fruit juice (about 8-10 fresh passion fruit)

To get the juice from the passion fruit, halve each fruit and scoop all the flesh and seeds into a small pan. Warm gently with 2 tablespoons of sugar. This helps to release the flesh from the seeds. Pass through a fine sieve,

165 g (5 oz) caster sugar
500 ml (17 fl oz) Vanilla
    Custard Sauce (see page
    181)
12 fresh kiwi
juice of 2 lemons

pressing the seeds hard to release all the juice and flesh.
You should have about 120 ml (4 fl oz) juice. Keep any
extra to drizzle over the finished dessert and keep some of
the seeds to decorate with as well.

Stir some of the juice into the cooled custard sauce to
taste. Remember to make it slightly extra tangy because
freezing will diminish the flavour.

Turn in an ice-cream machine following the manu-
facturer's instructions or freeze in a shallow tray, whisking
every 30 minutes to break up the ice crystals while
freezing.

Meanwhile, peel the kiwi fruit and place them in a
blender or food processor with the remaining sugar and
the lemon juice. Purée briefly. If it is left turning too long
the seeds will start to break up, discolouring the purée to
a muddy brown. Pass through a fine sieve. Return a
spoonful or two of the seeds to the purée and taste for
flavour. There should be about 500 ml (17 fl oz) of purée.
Chill in the fridge.

To serve, pour a generous ladle of the kiwi soup into
each soup plate. Place a scoop or two of the passion fruit
ice-cream in the centre and drizzle with a dash of passion
fruit juice. Decorate with a few passion fruit seeds
scattered over (they're totally edible).

OVERLEAF

*Meatless Meals, Menu 2: Mushroom and Aubergine Tart with
Garlic Chives (page 171); Penne with Broccoli, Goats' Cheese
and Sun-dried Tomatoes (page 172); Kiwi Soup with Passion
Fruit Ice-cream (page 172).*

CHAPTER 16

BASIC RECIPES

Th ese are useful basic recipes which you will need for several of the dishes in the book. They will also come in handy at other times when you are cooking.

SHORTCRUST PASTRY

This is a very workable shortcrust, not too short, yet crisp and tender. It is highly versatile as you can use it for almost any recipe, whether sweet or savoury. It's worth making in the quantity below and then freezing what you don't use the first time around.

MAKES ABOUT 900 G (2 LB)
675 g (1½ lb) soft flour
175 g (6 oz) caster sugar
350 g (12 oz) unsalted butter
3 eggs
dash of salt

You make this pastry by hand or by pulsing in a food processor. Place the flour and sugar in a chilled bowl. Add the butter and rub it in until the mixture is pea-size consistency. Stir together the eggs, pour into the bowl, add the salt and mix until the mixture comes together.

Transfer the mixture to your work surface and, using the heel of your hand, work the mixture until it all holds together in a cohesive ball and there are no big lumps of butter unmixed. Divide into four even batches, wrap well in cling film and chill. This pastry will keep in the fridge for about a week and in the freezer for about one month.

SAVOURY PASTRY

SAVOURY PASTRIES ARE THE BASE FOR SO MANY DISHES THAT IT'S REALLY WORTHWHILE TO PRACTISE WORKING WITH A SHORTCRUST DOUGH UNTIL YOU HAVE IT UNDER CONTROL.

MAKES ABOUT 900 G (2 LB)

450 g (1 lb) plain flour

25 g (1 oz) caster sugar

2 teaspoons salt

375 g (13 oz) unsalted butter, chilled and diced

2 eggs

2 tablespoons cream

You make this pastry by hand or by pulsing in a food processor. Place all the dry ingredients into a chilled bowl. Add the butter and rub it in until the mixture is pea-size consistency. Mix together the eggs and cream. Pour into the bowl and mix until the mixture comes together.

Transfer to your work surface and, with the heel of your hand, work until the mixture holds together nicely. Divide into three portions, wrap well in cling film and either chill or freeze. The pastry should be chilled for at least 1 hour before being used. This allows the butter to firm up and the flour to relax.

NOTE ON BAKING BLIND

Many recipes call for blind baking a tart base. This is simply a pre-baking of the base. It is accomplished by lining the base with greaseproof paper or kitchen foil and filling with beans of some sort. This holds the pastry in place until it has cooked enough to be set. The pastry is cooked with this blind bake in place for about 15 minutes at 190°C/375°F/gas 5. Often, after removing the beans and foil, the tart base is popped back into the oven for a minute or two to ensure that the bottom is evenly cooked to a golden brown.

A tip is to lightly brush the base and the sides of the cooked pastry with egg yolk to seal the pastry. This is especially helpful when the filling is a runny type - like the Lime Tart on page 29.

Standard Vinaigrette

Years ago people used vinaigrettes to dress salads and salads only. But now, realizing that they are tasty, healthy and open to endless variations of flavour, one finds them on vegetables, pastas, fish dishes, and so on. A good ratio to work to is one part vinegar to four or five parts oil. Keep all vinaigrettes in the fridge if they are not being used immediately, otherwise they can develop a rancid taste.

MAKES ABOUT 250 ML
(8 FL OZ)

1/2 teaspoon salt

1/2 teaspoon freshly ground
 pepper

2 teaspoons Dijon mustard

2-4 tablespoons white wine
 vinegar

230 ml (7 1/2 fl oz) olive oil,
 or vegetable oil

Dissolve the salt, pepper and mustard in the vinegar in a bowl. Whisk in the oil, slowly at first to allow it to be incorporated. Check and adjust the seasoning to taste. This can easily be made in a blender or food processor. Simply place all the ingredients in together, and blend.

CREAMY DILL DRESSING

A VERY SIMPLE AND REFINED SAUCE FOR SALADS OR FISH, THIS GOES VERY WELL WITH
SMOKED SALMON SALAD EXTRAVAGANZA (PAGE 20) OR SALMON TERRINE (PAGE 94).
THE SAUCE WILL KEEP FOR ABOUT TWO DAYS IN THE FRIDGE. IF YOU ARE MAKING IT
AHEAD DON'T ADD THE DILL UNTIL THE LAST MOMENT OR IT WILL DISCOLOUR.

MAKES ABOUT 250 ML
(8 FL OZ)

4 tablespoons lemon juice

2 teaspoons Dijon mustard

$\frac{1}{2}$ teaspoon salt

$\frac{1}{4}$ teaspoon freshly ground
white pepper

300 ml (10 fl oz) whipping
cream, chilled

3 tablespoons chopped fresh
dill

In a small bowl, whisk the lemon juice, mustard, salt and
pepper. Stir in the cream and chopped dill.

PASTRY CREAM

THIS PASTRY CREAM IS VERY THICK - REDUCING THE FLOUR OR CORNFLOUR WOULD LIGHTEN IT, BUT FOR OUR PURPOSES IN THIS BOOK WE NEED A THICKENED ONE. IT IS USED TO FILL ALL KINDS OF PASTRY DESSERTS FROM ÉCLAIRS TO PUFF PASTRIES AND TARTS. ITS VERSATILITY MAKES IT INVALUABLE IN DESSERT-MAKING SO PASTRY CREAM IS ONE TECHNIQUE THAT MUST BE MASTERED.

MAKES ABOUT 750 ML
(1¼ PINTS)

500 ml (17 fl oz) milk
½ vanilla pod
120 g (4½ oz) caster sugar
6 egg yolks
40 g (1½ oz) plain flour,
  sifted
20 g (¾ oz) cornflour, sifted
icing sugar (optional) to dust

Place the milk and vanilla pod in a pan and bring to the boil over a medium to high heat. Set aside to infuse.

Whisk together the sugar and egg yolks until they are light and pale yellow. Whisk in the flour and cornflour and continue to whisk well until smooth.

Slowly pour some of the hot milk on to the egg mixture, whisking continously. Pour in the rest of the milk and whisk to combine.

Return it all to the pan and cook over medium heat, whisking continuously for about 2-3 minutes until the mixture comes to the boil. Continue to whisk continuously and let it cook for another 2 minutes. This ensures that the raw flour is cooked. Remove from the heat.

Strain through a fine sieve into a clean bowl. The vanilla pod can be removed at this stage as most of the seeds will already have been released into the pastry cream. Either cover with a layer of cling film right on top of the pastry cream or heavily dust the top with icing sugar. Either method helps prevent a crust from forming while cooling. When cool the pastry cream can be stored in the fridge for up to five days.

VANILLA CUSTARD SAUCE

Simple vanilla custard sauce, or crème anglaise, is an essential recipe for anyone interested in pastry and dessert-making. You can build various flavours and spices into this base recipe. Most, like coconut or cinnamon, are infused in the milk before the custard is made. But remember, alcohol and honey should be added only after the custard has been cooked and cooled slightly. This custard can keep in the fridge for up to five days depending on how fresh the milk was to start with.

MAKES ABOUT 600 ML (1 PINT)
500 ml (17 fl oz) whole milk
½ vanilla pod, split or ½
teaspoon vanilla essence
6 large egg yolks
120 g (4 ½ oz) caster sugar

Place the milk in a pan with the vanilla pod and bring to the boil. Set aside to infuse.

Whisk the egg yolks and sugar together in a bowl until lightened in colour and the sugar has dissolved. Whisking continuously, slowly pour the milk into the egg yolk and sugar mixture and whisk together. Pour this mixture back into the pan and cook over a low heat, stirring continuously with a wooden spoon until the mixture has thickened enough to coat the back of the spoon and will hold if you run your finger along the middle of the back of the spoon.

When it is to desired thickness, strain through a fine mesh sieve and cool. You can leave the vanilla pod in the anglaise to continue to increase the flavour or remove at this point scraping all the seeds from the inside of the pod into the custard.

BRANDIED APRICOT SAUCE

THIS SAUCE CAN BE KEPT FOR UP TO TWO WEEKS IN AN AIRTIGHT CONTAINER IN THE FRIDGE.

MAKES ABOUT 400 ML (14 FL OZ)

200-250 g (7-9 oz) good
  quality dried apricots
juice of 1 lemon
500 ml (17 fl oz) water
200 g (7 oz) caster sugar
100 ml (3½ fl oz) brandy

Place the dried apricots, lemon juice, water and sugar in a pan. Bring to the boil and let simmer gently for about 30 minutes or until the apricots are very soft. Remove from heat and leave to cool slightly.

Purée in a blender or food processor and pass through a fine sieve. Taste to check sweetness/tartness and add the brandy.

BLACKCURRANT SAUCE

MAKES ABOUT 400 G (14 FL OZ)

250 g (9 oz) frozen
   blackcurrants, defrosted
5 tablespoons water
150 g (5 oz) caster sugar
1-2 teaspoons lemon juice

Simply place all the ingredients in a blender or food processor and process. Pass though a fine sieve and taste for flavour. Adjust with more sugar or lemon juice as necessary. Set aside.

CHOCOLATE SAUCE

HERE IS A SIMPLE CHOCOLATE SAUCE THAT'S EASY TO WHIP UP AND KEEPS VERY WELL IN AN AIRTIGHT CONTAINER IN THE FRIDGE FOR A WEEK TO TEN DAYS. YOU CAN FLAVOUR IT WITH A LIQUEUR IF YOU WISH.

MAKES ABOUT 250 ML (8 FL OZ)

150 ml (5 fl oz) milk
50 ml (2 fl oz) whipping
   cream
250 g (9 oz) plain chocolate,
   finely chopped or grated

Bring the milk and cream to the boil. Remove from heat and leave to cool slightly. Stir in the finely chopped chocolate. Stir until well mixed and all the chocolate has melted.

To re-heat the sauce melt in a bowl over a pan of simmering water, or at about half power in the microwave for 1-2 minutes.

TOFFEE SAUCE

A MULTI-PURPOSE TOFFEE SAUCE WITH A REAL BUTTERSCOTCH FLAVOUR, THIS GOES WITH SO MANY THINGS IT IS EXCELLENT FOR ANY PASTRY CHEF'S REPERTOIRE. THE SAUCE CAN BE USED WARM OR COLD. IT KEEPS WELL IN THE FRIDGE FOR UP TO TWO WEEKS.

MAKES ABOUT 250 ML (8 FL OZ)

150 g (5 oz) light soft brown sugar

120 ml (4 fl oz) double cream

120 g (5 oz) unsalted butter

1 teaspoon vanilla essence

Bring all ingredients to the boil together in a pan over a medium to high heat and cook for 2 minutes, stirring continuously. The colour will change to a rich golden hue. Remove from the heat and leave to cool.

INDEX OF RECIPE TYPES

Titles in italics are vegetarian recipes.

INDEX